easy
gourmet

PAGE STREET
PUBLISHING CO.

First published in 2014 by

Page Street Publishing Co.

27 Congress Street, Suite 103

Salem, MA 01970

www.pagestreetpublishing.com

Distributed by Macmillan; sales in Canada by The Canadian Manda Group; distribution in Canada by The Jaguar Book Group.

17   16   15   14   2   3   4   5

ISBN-13: 978-1-62414-062-4

ISBN-10: 1-62414-062-9

Library of Congress Control Number: 2013922836

Cover and book design by Stephanie Le

Photography by Stephanie Le

Printed and bound in China

Page Street is proud to be a member of 1% for the Planet. Members donate one percent of their sales to one or more of the over 1,500 environmental and sustainability charities across the globe who participate in this program.

easy gourmet

AWESOME RECIPES *anyone* CAN COOK

from the creator of

i am a food blog

named Top Cooking Blog by *Saveur* magazine

STEPHANIE LE

PAGE STREET
PUBLISHING CO.

To Mike: for then, for now and for always

I never used to like eating, which is a strange admission for a now avid food lover and cook, but when I was a child, I was the pickiest eater around. I would drive my parents crazy with the things that I would and wouldn't eat.

My food choices were never logical—they were based on whimsy and, more often than not, the people around me. Once, at daycare, a boy pointed at my lunch of soy sauce fried noodles and yelled, loud enough for the 5-year-olds to hear in the next room, "Stephanie's eating wooooooorms!" Tears immediately started pouring down my face and even though minutes before I was looking forward to digging into what was one of my favorite foods, I suddenly couldn't stand to have them near me. In hindsight, I should have said, "spaghetti's worms too!" but my 3-year-old brain wasn't too quick with the comebacks.

Instead, being the sensitive kid that I was, I told my mom that I was never going to eat Chinese food again. My mom made a deal with me: at home I'd eat whatever she put on the table, but for daycare lunches she'd make more "kid appropriate" (read: boring lunches). I wanted to be just like everyone else, so I agreed.

My mom wasn't the type to go by the book, so it wasn't long before my lunches were legendary. Kids always wanted to trade with me and I happily gave away my thermoses of homemade chicken noodle soup, cup of cut fruit and freshly baked chocolate chip cookies for store-bought lunchables, chips and canned peaches.

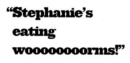

"Stephanie's eating wooooooorms!"

Eventually, my taste buds grew up and I went from being extremely picky to eating almost everything. What changed was being exposed to a whole other world of food beyond the predominately Asian food we ate at home. I'd go out for a bite to eat and absolutely fall in love with all the flavors. In an attempt to be able to eat all the dishes I fell in love with (while still in my pyjamas), I started cooking in earnest. I experimented with recreating and creating dishes and eventually started I Am a Food Blog to record my efforts.

Everyone's definition of good food is different, but one thing holds true across the table: sharing a meal brings people together. Eating, laughing and lingering over a good meal is my idea of a really good time. Eating together and enjoying that particular moment at that particular time with the people you choose makes memories you just won't forget.

Easy Gourmet contains some of my favorite recipes. And they are meant to be just that: easy, yet unexpectedly delicious. Coconut Carrot soup gets a kick from a red curry paste, and Baked Mac & Cheese is fancied up with Gruyère and Swiss. The recipes are as eclectic as my taste in food. A little bit Asian, a little bit classic and a lot delicious, these recipes are what I love to cook.

BREAKFAST

Breakfast holds a special place in my heart. I have fond memories of sitting around my family's old marble laminate table, waiting anxiously for my mom to finish frying eggs to have with bacon and toast. Hot breakfasts were reserved for the weekends, when my mom actually had time to make all the good stuff. During the week, my mom worked the graveyard shift and we made do with cereal and milk, so weekends were the best thing ever.

As I grew up, I became obsessed with cooking breakfast, no matter what the time of day. I'd whip up plates of pancakes for dinner or omelettes for lunch. There's probably nothing easier or more rewarding than learning how to cook breakfast. Typical breakfast foods can and should be anytime foods, especially if they're Blueberry Waffles, Pulled Pork Pancakes or Chicken & Waffles.

CHICKEN & WAFFLES

SERVES: 4-6

A CLASSIC SOUTHERN BREAKFAST COMBINATION

Chicken and Waffles are one of those dishes I always order if I see it on the menu. I love the contrast of sweet and savory, fluffy and crispy. Some might call it blasphemy, but I think it's even better when the chicken is boneless so I don't have to slow down when eating. Using chicken breast strips in this recipe doubles the goodness: the strips cook up fast and you can roll everything up into a handheld waffle taco.

INGREDIENTS

3 _____ large chicken breasts, cut into 1-inch (2.5-cm) strips

1 ½ cups (210 g) _____ all-purpose flour
2 tsp (6 g) _____ garlic powder
2 tsp (6 g) _____ onion powder
1 tsp (2 g) _____ paprika
1 tsp (4 g) _____ cayenne
1 tsp (8 g) _____ salt
1 tsp (2 g) _____ freshly ground pepper

2 cups (280 g) _____ all purpose flour
2 tbsp (30 g) _____ sugar
2 tsp (8 g) _____ baking powder
1 tsp (8 g) _____ baking soda
pinch _____ salt

2 cups (480 ml) _____ buttermilk
6 tbsp (170 g) _____ butter, melted
2 _____ large eggs

to serve _____ syrup, if desired

METHOD

Soak chicken strips in the buttermilk, salt and pepper for 15-20 minutes. Combine the flour, garlic and onion powder, paprika and cayenne in a large bowl.

Heat up 1-inch (2.5-cm) of oil to 350°F (180°C) in a deep skillet over medium heat. While the oil is heating, take a strip of chicken from the buttermilk and place it in the coating, turning to coat completely. Coat the chicken right before you add it to the hot oil.

Cook the strips a few at a time until golden brown and crispy, about 1 ½-2 minutes per side. When cooked, remove and drain on paper towels. Keep strips warm in the oven while making the waffles.

Preheat your waffle iron. In a bowl, mix together the dry ingredients. In another bowl, whisk together the melted butter, milk and eggs. Add the wet ingredients to the dry, stirring until just combined.

Grease your waffle iron if needed and cook waffles according to waffle iron instructions or until the waffles are golden brown and crispy. Keep waffles warm in the oven in a single layer on a cooling rack placed inside a baking tray. Continuing waffling until you finish the batter.

Serve fried chicken on top of waffles with your favorite syrup.

CHICKEN &
WAFFLES

CARROT CAKE PANCAKES

WITH VANILLA MASCARPONE & TOASTED WALNUTS

CARROT CAKE PANCAKES

SERVES: 4

CARROT-FILLED PANCAKES WITH VANILLA MASCARPONE

Did you know that eating too many carrots will make your skin literally turn orange? When I was four, I was in danger of just that, as I spent months consuming massive amounts of carrots. I was convinced that I was a bona fide bunny and eating carrots would give me better night vision. I was wrong on both counts, but to this day I still hold carrots near and dear to my heart. These fluffy pancakes taste just like carrot cake, and incorporate three of my favorite things: carrots, breakfast and dessert.

INGREDIENTS

1 cup (140 g) _____ all-purpose flour
1 tsp (4 g) _____ baking powder
1 tsp (8 g) _____ baking soda
1 tbsp (15 g) _____ sugar
¼ tsp _____ salt
½ tsp _____ cinnamon
¼ tsp _____ nutmeg
⅛ tsp _____ ground ginger
1 cup (120 g) _____ finely grated carrots
1 _____ large egg
1 cup (240 ml) _____ buttermilk

½ cup (110 g) _____ mascarpone, room temp
2 tbsp (30 g) _____ sugar
½ cup (120 ml) _____ heavy whipping cream
1 tsp (5 ml) _____ vanilla

¼ cup (30 g) _____ walnut pieces, if desired
as needed _____ butter or oil for pan

METHOD

In a large bowl, whisk together the flour, baking powder, baking soda, sugar, salt, cinnamon, nutmeg, ginger and carrots. In a separate bowl, whisk together the egg and buttermilk. Add the wet ingredients to the dry and mix until just combined. Let batter sit for 10 minutes while making the vanilla mascarpone.

In a bowl, cream together the mascarpone and sugar until the sugar is dissolved. In a separate bowl, whip up the whipping cream until it thickens and holds medium peaks (when you lift the whisk from the cream, the tip of the peak will curl over on itself). Gently fold together the mascarpone-sugar mixture with the whipping cream and mix in the vanilla. Set aside in the fridge.

Toast the walnuts in a dry, heavy skillet over medium heat for 1-2 minutes while stirring constantly. Set aside while making the pancakes.

Heat a nonstick frying pan over medium-low heat. Brush a thin layer of butter or oil on your pan. Drop the batter 2 tablespoons (30 ml) at a time into the pan. Cook until tiny bubbles appear on the surface, about 2-3 minutes. Flip and continue cooking for 1-2 minutes. Keep the pancakes in the warm oven until you're done with the batter.

Top the pancakes with vanilla mascarpone and toasted walnuts, if desired.

SPICY SHRIMP OMELETTE

SERVES: 2

A SOUTHEAST ASIAN TAKE ON A CLASSIC OMELETTE

I never used to like spicy food, so when my parents hoarded their chili sauce, it wasn't a big deal. Now that I've turned into a spice fiend though, going over to my parents' house for breakfast is a more interesting affair. My mom will hide her specialty sambals way in the back of the fridge, in hopes that I won't find them — but I always do. Spice just makes breakfast so much more nice and this shrimp omelette with lime and cilantro will wake up your taste buds in the best way possible.

INGREDIENTS

12 _____ large shrimp, peeled & deveined

1 tsp (5 ml) ____ sambal oelek (chili garlic sauce)

juice _____ of ½ lime

1 tsp (5 g) _____ sugar

1 tsp (5 ml) _____ fish sauce

1 _____ green onion, sliced

2 tbsp (2.5 g) _____ chopped cilantro

1 ½ tbsp (23 ml) _____ oil, divided

4 _____ large eggs

2 tsp (10 ml) _ sambal oelek (chili garlic sauce)

¼ tsp _____ salt

1 _____ green onion, sliced

½ cup (20 g) _____ chopped cilantro

to serve _____ lime wedges

METHOD

In a bowl, marinate the shrimp for 15 minutes in the sambal, lime juice, sugar, fish sauce, green onions and cilantro. Set aside.

In another bowl, beat together the eggs, samal oelek and salt.

Heat up ½ tablespoon (8 ml) of oil in a small nonstick skillet over medium-high heat. Add the shrimp and cook until pink and slightly charred, 1 to 2 minutes per side. Remove from the pan and set aside.

Heat up ½ tablespoon (8 ml) of oil in the pan over medium heat and add half of the eggs. Swirl the eggs in the pan, and with a rubber spatula, gently move cooked eggs to the center of the pan, swirling to move uncooked eggs to replace. When the eggs look about 60% cooked, add 6 shrimp, a sprinkle of green onions and cilantro leaves. Use the spatula to fold the omelette in half. Serve immediately for ultimate deliciousness or keep warm in a 200°F (93°C) oven while making the second omelette. To serve, top with more green onions, cilantro and a lime wedge.

PEACHES & CREAM FRENCH TOAST

SERVES: 2

CINNAMON TOAST, PEACH BOURBON SYRUP & VANILLA MASCARPONE

French toast is super easy to make and one of the first things I learned how to cook. I started out with your basic day-old bread dipped into eggs, but it wasn't long before I started experimenting with all sorts of fruits and flavors. One of my favorite combinations is peaches and cream. Warm peaches and cool mascarpone on top of crisp and creamy toast is supremely addictive. Top it all off with a bourbon sauce, and you have yourself a definite winner.

INGREDIENTS

½ cup (112 g) _____ mascarpone, room temp
2 tbsp (30 g) _____ sugar
½ cup (120 ml) _____ heavy whipping cream
1 tsp (5 ml) _____ vanilla

2 _____ large eggs
⅓ cup (80 ml) _____ milk
1 tsp (2 g) _____ cinnamon
4 thick slices _____ day old French bread
1 tbsp (15 g) _____ butter

¼ cup (55 g) _____ brown sugar
2 tbsp (30 g) _____ white sugar
¼ cup (60 ml) _____ bourbon
½ cup (120 ml) _____ water
2 _____ peaches, sliced

METHOD

In a bowl, cream together the mascarpone and sugar until sugar is dissolved. Whip the whipping cream until it thickens and holds medium peaks. (When you lift the whisk from the cream, the tip of the peak will curl over on itself.) Gently fold together the mascarpone-sugar mixture, cream and vanilla. Set aside in the fridge.

Beat eggs, milk and cinnamon together in a shallow bowl. Dip slices of bread into egg mix, flipping once. Melt the butter in a large nonstick skillet over medium to medium-high heat. Add the soaked slices of bread and fry until golden brown on both sides, flipping once, 2-3 minutes per side.

While the toast is cooking, make the peach bourbon syrup. In a small saucepan, bring the sugars, bourbon and water to a boil over high heat. Turn the heat down to medium-low, add the peaches and let the syrup bubble gently. Reduce to a syrup-like consistency, about 5-6 minutes.

Top toast with the bourbon peaches and vanilla mascarpone.

CINNAMON FRENCH TOAST

Peaches & Cream

W/ PEACH BOURBON SYRUP

POTATOES & EGGS

SERVES: 4-6

SPANISH EGG OMELETTE WITH POTATOES AND ONIONS

I spent one summer in Spain consuming entirely too many eggs and potatoes. It was all because I started every day with a slice of Spanish tortilla. Although Spanish and Mexican tortillas share the same name, the similarities end there. Spanish tortillas are delicious, massive omelettes filled with potatoes and onions. They're eaten hot or cold, day or night, with or without bread. I like them at room temperature with a little hot sauce.

INGREDIENTS

1 cup (240 ml) _____ olive oil

1 small _____ onion, thinly sliced

2 cups (360 g) _____ Yukon gold potatoes, peeled and thinly sliced

5 _____ large eggs

¼ tsp _____ salt

⅛ tsp _____ freshly ground pepper

METHOD

In an 8-inch (20-cm) nonstick frying pan, heat oil over medium heat. Add the onions and potatoes. Cook over medium heat until the potatoes are cooked through and soft, about 12-15 minutes. The oil should never be hot enough to fry the potatoes or turn them brown; the goal is gentle bubbles. When the potatoes are tender, turn off the heat and let potatoes and onions cool for 10 minutes. While cooling, beat eggs in a large bowl and season with salt and pepper. Use a slotted spoon to remove the potatoes and onions from oil, placing them in a bowl with the eggs. (Be sure to save the oil.) Let the potatoes sit for up to an hour in the eggs for an extra-creamy tortilla.

Heat up 2 tablespoons (30 ml) of the reserved oil over low heat. Add the potato-egg mixture and cook for 10-12 minutes. Use a rubber spatula to check if the bottom is slightly browned; the top will be still be runny. Invert the tortilla onto a rimless plate and slide back into the pan to cook for 3-5 more minutes. Let rest for 10 minutes and serve warm or at room temperature.

SPANISH STYLE
POTATOES
AND
EGGS
=

PULLED PORK PANCAKES

SERVES: 4

PULLED PORK, BUTTERMILK PANCAKES & BOURBON SYRUP

There's a supremely popular restaurant in Vancouver that specializes in brunch. I generally don't mind a bit of a wait for good food, but lines out the door and wait times of over an hour and a half are a bit much, even for me. Sometimes, though, waiting is worth it when you come across that genius restaurant dish that seems easy enough to make at home. After tasting pulled pork pancakes myself, I tried my hand at making my own, and once I figured out the recipe, there was no looking back.

INGREDIENTS

1 cup (140 g)	all-purpose flour
1 tsp (4 g)	baking powder
1 tsp (8 g)	baking soda
1 tsp (5 g)	sugar
1	large egg
1 cup (240 ml)	buttermilk
as needed	oil or butter for pan
2 cups (400 g)	pulled pork (page 88), warmed
½ cup (110 g)	brown sugar
¼ cup (50 g)	white sugar
¼ cup (60 ml)	bourbon
½ cup (120 ml)	water

METHOD

Preheat the oven to 225°F (110°C). Mix together the flour, baking powder, baking soda and sugar in a large bowl. In a small bowl, beat the egg and then mix with the buttermilk. Add the wet ingredients to the flour mixture and stir until just combined. Let batter sit for 10 minutes.

Heat up a nonstick frying pan over medium-low heat. Brush a thin layer of butter or oil on the pan. Drop the batter 2 tablespoons (30 ml) at a time into the pan. Cook until tiny bubbles appear on the surface, about 2-3 minutes. Flip and continue cooking for 1-2 minutes. Keep the pancakes in the warm oven until you're done with the batter.

To make the bourbon syrup, bring the sugars, bourbon and water to a boil in a small saucepan over high heat. Turn the heat to medium-low and let the syrup bubble gently and reduce until it reaches a syrup-like consistency, about 5-6 minutes. Let stand 5 minutes.

To serve, top pancakes with pulled pork. Serve with warm bourbon syrup.

PULLED PORK
PANCAKES
BOURBON SYRUP

BACON & CHEDDAR
·POTATO WAFFLES·
· A BRUNCH FAVORITE ·

POTATO WAFFLES

SERVES: 4-6

POTATO WAFFLES WITH BACON, CHEDDAR & GREEN ONIONS

I generally overestimate how much I think people will eat, so I always end up making massive amounts of food. Thankfully, I love leftovers. They're perfect for when you're too hungry to cook. Even better, though, is taking leftovers and making them into something else entirely. Leftover mashed potatoes can be the base for so many delicious new things. Take these mashed potato waffles—they're even more delicious because they're so easy to make. Leftover mashed potatoes always lead to good things.

INGREDIENTS

2 tbsp (30 ml) _____ oil

¼ cup (60 ml) _____ buttermilk

2 _____ large eggs

2 ½ cups (525 g) _____ mashed potatoes

½ cup (40 g) _____ sliced green onions

1 cup (275 g) _____ cooked bacon,
chopped into ½-inch (1.3-cm) pieces

1 cup (110 g) _____ grated cheddar cheese

½ cup (70 g) _____ all-purpose flour

½ tsp _____ baking powder

¼ tsp _____ baking soda

½ tsp _____ salt

½ tsp _____ freshly ground pepper

METHOD

Preheat your waffle maker. Preheat the oven to 225°F (110°C).

In a large bowl, whisk together the wet ingredients: oil, buttermilk and eggs. Add the mashed potatoes, green onions, bacon and cheddar cheese. Mix well.

In a small bowl, mix together the dry ingredients: flour, baking powder, baking soda, salt and pepper.

Add the dry ingredients to the wet ingredients and mix gently until just combined.

Grease your waffle iron if needed and cook waffles according to waffle iron instructions or until the waffles are golden brown and crispy. Keep waffles warm in the oven in a single layer on a cooling rack placed inside a baking tray. Continuing waffling until you finish the batter. Enjoy the waffles warm with syrup, if desired.

SAUTÉED SPINACH

CODDLED EGGS

CREAMY MASH

CODDLED EGGS

SERVES: 2

SOFTLY STEAMED EGGS, MASHED POTATOES & SAUTÉED SPINACH

Did you ever have toast and soldiers when you were a kid? Growing up, crunchy buttered toast dipped into a soft-boiled egg was a special treat for me. I know now that it was also a treat for my busy mom: eggs and toast were simple to make, easy to eat and delicious. This is my grown-up version of that classic childhood breakfast. It's perfect for customization, so forget what your parents told you and play with your food!

INGREDIENTS

1 cup (30 g) _____ raw spinach

as needed _____ oil

to taste _____ salt & freshly ground pepper

1 tsp (5 g) _____ butter for the ramekins

½ cup (105 g) _____ mashed potatoes

2 _____ large eggs, room temp

1 tsp (1 g) _____ chopped flat-leaf parsley

METHOD

In a kettle or pot, bring a generous amount of water to a boil.

While the water is boiling, sauté the spinach in a touch of oil over medium heat until just wilted, 1-2 minutes. Season with salt and pepper and remove from the pan.

Grease two ramekins with the butter. Divide the potatoes between them. Top the potatoes with the wilted spinach. Gently place the raw eggs onto the spinach.

Place the ramekins in a deep roasting pan. Pour enough hot water into the pan to come up halfway up the sides of the ramekins.

Carefully put the tray on the center rack of the oven. Bake until the whites are gently set and the yolks are still runny, about 17-20 minutes. Carefully remove ramekins, sprinkle with flat-leaf parsley and serve with plenty of buttered toast.

QUINOA PEA CAKES

SERVES: 2-4

CRISPY QUINOA PEA CILANTRO CAKES

Quinoa is a superfood and super healthy for you, but I mostly like it because it just tastes good. The nuttiness and texture of fluffy quinoa is great on its own, but even better when made into a little cake and pan fried. I like making tiny versions of these cakes and dipping them in sriracha as a snack, but if you want to be a bit fancier you can make the cakes bigger and top them off with a fried egg yolk for a special brunch treat.

INGREDIENTS

1 cup (170 g) _____ quinoa
1 ½ cups (360 ml) _____ chicken/vegetable stock
1 cup (130 g) ___ frozen peas, cooked & drained
⅓ cup (30 g) _____ finely grated parmesan
⅓ cup (13 g) _____ chopped cilantro
¼ cup (15 g) _____ panko or bread crumbs
¼ tsp _____ salt
¼ tsp _____ freshly ground pepper
4 _____ large eggs
as needed _____ oil for pan
if desired _____ eggs to top

METHOD

Rinse the quinoa in a fine mesh sieve until the water runs clear. Place in a pot and toast for a minute over medium heat while stirring. Add the stock and bring to a roiling boil. Lower the heat to the lowest setting, cover the pot. Cook until quinoa is tender and you can see curlicues around the edges of the grain, 25-30 minutes. Remove from heat and let stand for 5 minutes. Fluff and cool.

When the quinoa is cool, stir in the peas, parmesan, cilantro, panko, salt and pepper. Stir in the eggs until completely incorporated.

Form ⅓-cup (50-g) cakes. Heat up a bit of oil in a large nonstick frying pan. Fry cakes over medium heat until golden, 8-10 minutes per side.

If topping with a fried yolk, crack the egg into a small dish and pour off the white. Save whites for another use. Gently tip the yolk into a frying pan with a bit of oil. Fry over medium heat for about 1 minute. Place on top of the quinoa cake and enjoy immediately.

BLUEBERRY WAFFLES

SERVES: 4

CRISP & CHEWY BLUEBERRY WAFFLES MADE WITH SWEET RICE FLOUR

It sounds strange, but when I visit Japan, I always have brunch at one of the many cafes that boast American-style waffles and pancakes. Between the strange combinations, like curry on waffles, you'll find delicious interpretations you'd never get at home, like mochi and blueberries. Mochiko flour, carried at most American grocery stores, gives these waffles a pleasant chewiness. Not too sweet, with a crisp exterior and chewy interior, these blueberry mochi waffles are the best kind of fusion.

INGREDIENTS

1 cup (140 g)	all-purpose flour
1 cup (170 g)	mochiko flour
¼ tsp	salt
¼ cup (50 g)	sugar
3 tsp (10 g)	baking powder
1 ½ cups (360 ml)	milk
2	large eggs
1 cup (170 g)	blueberries
to serve	syrup, if desired

METHOD

Preheat the waffle iron. Preheat the oven to 225°F (107°C).

In a large bowl, stir together the flour, mochiko, salt, sugar and baking powder. In a liquid measuring cup, whisk the milk and eggs together. Add the wet ingredients to the dry ingredients and mix until just incorporated. Gently stir in the blueberries.

Grease your waffle iron if needed and cook waffles according to waffle iron instructions or until the waffles are golden brown and crispy. Keep waffles warm in the oven in a single layer on a cooling rack placed inside a baking tray. Continuing waffling until you finish the batter. Enjoy the waffles warm with syrup.

BREAKFAST SCONES

MAKES: ABOUT 18 SCONES

SAVORY SCONES WITH JALAPEÑOS, BACON & CHEDDAR

Long ago, I used to work the counter at a bakery where they made cheddar cheese and green onion scones. I loved the smell of those scones coming out of the oven and would always hope there would be a tiny one on the tray made just for me. These scones have the added bonus of crispy bacon bits and spicy jalapeños. They remind me of cold, clear mornings and the hopefulness of deserted spaces waiting for people to rush in for their morning treats.

INGREDIENTS

8 slices	thick-cut bacon
2 cups (280 g)	all-purpose flour
2 tsp (8 g)	baking powder
¼ tsp	salt
½ tsp	freshly ground pepper
½ cup (115 g)	cold butter, cut into chunks
2	small jalapeños, minced
1 ½ cups (165 g)	shredded chedda , divided
1	large egg
¾ cups (180 ml)	heavy cream or whole milk
1	large egg beaten with 1 tsp (5 ml) water

METHOD

Preheat the oven to 400°F(205°C). Line a rimmed baking sheet with parchment paper.

Chop the bacon into ½-inch (1.3-cm) pieces and cook in a small skillet over medium-low heat until crisp and deeply browned. Remove from the skillet, drain and cool on paper towels.

In a large bowl, mix together the flour, baking powder and salt. Using a fork or pastry cutter, cut the butter into the flour mixture until it resembles very coarse meal. Stir in the jalapeños, 1 cup (110 g) cheddar and cooked bacon.

In a small bowl, whisk together the egg and cream or milk until well blended. Pour the egg mixture into the dry ingredients and mix until everything comes together. The dough will be quite sticky.

Turn the dough onto a lightly floured work surface and gently pat the dough to 1-inch (2.5-cm) thickness. Using a 1 ½-inch (3.8-cm) round or square cookie cutter, cut out as many scones as possible, placing them evenly on the prepared baking sheet. Gather scraps, pat gently and cut out more scones. Brush with egg wash and sprinkle the tops with the remaining ½ cup (55 g) of cheddar and bake until the scones are golden, about 12-15 minutes. Transfer the scones to a wire rack, cool slightly and serve.

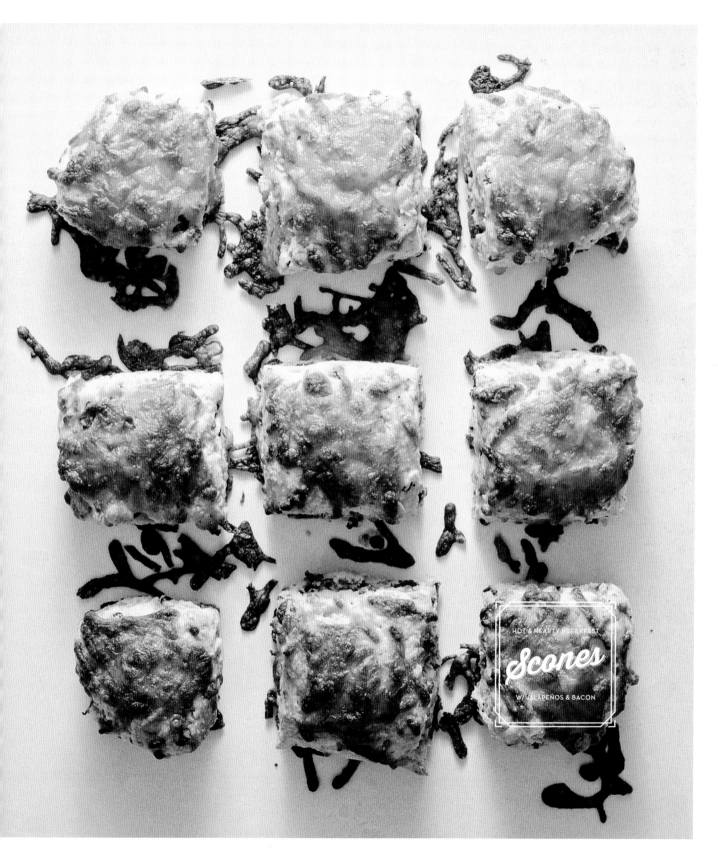

HOT & HEARTY BREAKFAST

Scones

W/ JALAPEÑOS & BACON

SOY MILK DOUGHNUTS

MAKES: 6 DOUGHNUTS

OVEN-BAKED DOUGHNUTS WITH A HINT OF SWEETNESS

Many of my favorite things to make at home have been inspired by travelling. I love discovering unique flavor combinations and new takes on old favorites. These baked soy milk doughnuts are delightfully light, moist and addictive. Baking doughnuts is a tiny bit healthier than frying, but the true bonus is whenever I bite into one of these warm doughnuts, it takes me right back to Kyoto, where I ate tiny soy milk doughnuts by the handful.

INGREDIENTS

1 cup (140 g) _____ all-purpose flour

2 tsp (8 g) _____ baking powder

¼ tsp _____ salt

¼ cup (50 g) _____ sugar

2 tbsp (30 ml) _____ honey

1 _____ large egg, room temp

3 tbsp (45 ml) _____ oil

¼ cup plus 2 tbsp (90 ml) _____ soy milk

METHOD

Preheat the oven to 400°F (205°C). Lightly grease a nonstick 6-count doughnut pan. Whisk together the flour, baking powder, and salt in a large bowl. In a small bowl, whisk the sugar, egg, oil, soy milk and honey. Add the wet ingredients to the dry and stir until just combined. Fill each well of the pan ¾ full. Bake for 11-12 minutes, until golden and an inserted toothpick comes out dry. Let cool for 5 minutes before turning out onto a cooling rack. Enjoy immediately while still warm.

SOY MILK
DOUGHNUTS

PASTA & RICE

Carbs are delicious. There's no denying that digging into a giant bowl of pasta or rice is the ultimate in comfort. It's like slipping into your favorite super-cozy, oversized fall sweater, and just like sweaters, starches are pretty forgiving. You don't need to do much to make them taste fantastic, but when you do dress them up, they really shine. I love carbs so much that while most people are eating fresh summer strawberries or the first asparagus of year, you'll find me tucking into a bowl of Scallop Fried Rice, Baked Mac & Cheese or a big plate of Spaghetti & Meatballs. Starches know that they don't need to be trendy; just like your favorite sweater, they're a perennial staple.

PEA & BACON RISOTTO

SERVES: 2-3

CREAMY RICE, CRISP BACON, PEAS

Creamy and comforting, risotto is one of the best things you'll ever learn how to cook. The first time I made risotto I stirred until my arm was about to fall off. It took forever until my rice was al dente and creamy. I later realized that heating the stock before stirring it into the rice is key, as is toasting your rice kernels. Once you have the technique down, risotto is quick and easy to make. If you leave out the peas and bacon in this recipe, you'll have a blank slate risotto that you can customize as you please.

INGREDIENTS

4 ½ cups (1 l) _____ chicken stock

1 tbsp (15 g) _____ butter

1 tsp (5 ml) _____ oil

1 cup (228 g) _____ arborio rice

½ _____ small onion, diced

½ cup (64 g) _____ frozen peas, thawed

4 slices _____ cooked thick-cut bacon, in 1-inch (2.5-cm) pieces

¼ cup (45 g) _____ freshly grated parmesan

to taste _____ salt & freshly ground pepper

METHOD

In a medium stockpot, heat the stock to a gentle simmer.

Melt the butter with the oil in a medium saucepan over medium heat. Add the diced onions and cook until translucent, 1-2 minutes. Turn the heat up to medium-high and add the rice. Toast the rice, about 3-4 minutes, until slightly translucent.

Turn the heat down to medium and add a ladle of hot stock. Stir into the rice until the liquid is mostly absorbed. Continue stirring and adding hot stock as the rice absorbs it. Taste after about 15 minutes. If the rice is soft but with a bit of bite, it's ready. If still uncooked, continue adding stock a ladle at a time. When done, remove from the heat and stir in the peas, bacon and cheese. Taste and season with salt and pepper. Enjoy immediately.

SPAGHETTI & MEATBALLS

SERVES: 4-6

PORK MEATBALLS WITH CRUSHED FENNEL SEEDS & FLAT-LEAF PARSLEY

Apparently, spaghetti and meatballs is not a thing in Italy. I'm not sure how that's possible as it's hard to resist a good meatball. These fennel pork meatballs are definitely irresistible. Light, yet satisfying, pork meatballs are a bit different than your everyday beef variety, but are just as easy to make. The fennel seeds add a pleasant crunch and a slight anise flavor that perfectly complements the pork. They taste great on their own, tossed with basic tomato sauce and pasta or even on pizza.

INGREDIENTS

2 tbsp (30 ml) _____ oil

1 ½ tsp (3 g) _____ crushed red pepper

½ _____ yellow onion, finely chopped

2 _____ garlic cloves, finely chopped

¼ cup (30 g) _____ finely shredded carrot
(about ½ medium carrot)

1 28-oz (828 ml) can ____ crushed red tomatoes

½ tsp _____ salt

3 tbsp (45 ml) _____ oil, divided

½ _____ onion, finely diced

2 tsp (4 g) _____ fennel seeds, crushed

1 lb (450 g) _____ ground pork

2 tbsp (7.5 g) _____ roughly chopped
flat-leaf parsley

3 tbsp (11.25 g) _____ panko/breadcrumbs

1 _____ large egg

½ tsp _____ salt

½ tsp _____ freshly ground pepper

8-10 oz (225-280 g) _____ spaghetti

METHOD

To make the sauce, heat the oil in a medium saucepan over medium heat. Add the crushed red pepper, onion, garlic and carrots and stir to coat. Reduce the heat to low and cook until everything is softened but not browned, about 10 minutes. Stir in the tomatoes and salt and bring to a gentle simmer, uncovered. Simmer for 30 minutes until the sauce has thickened slightly. Remove from the heat and taste to see if you need more salt.

In a small saucepan, heat up 1 tablespoon (15 ml) oil over medium heat. Add the onions and fennel seeds and stir to coat. Cook until the onions are translucent and slightly brown, about 6-8 minutes. Remove the onions and fennel seeds from the pan, set aside to cool.

In a large bowl, combine the ground pork, parsley, panko, egg, salt and pepper, along with the cooled onion and fennel seed mixture. Mix well and shape into 1-inch (2.5-cm) size meatballs (about 2 tablespoons [27 g] each). Heat remaining 2 tablespoons (30 ml) of oil in a large skillet over medium-high heat until hot and shimmery. Add the meatballs to the pan, being careful not to overcrowd. Turn the heat to medium and brown the meatballs on all sides, turning as needed, about 4-5 minutes per side, 20 minutes total. Add the meatballs to the sauce and simmer for 10 minutes.

Cook the spaghetti according to the package. Drain and serve with meatballs and sauce.

FENNEL PORK MEATBALLS

SPAGHETTI WITH TOMATO

BAKED MAC & CHEESE

SERVES: 4-6

BUBBLY, GOLDEN CHEESE, CREAMY SAUCE & TENDER NOODLES

My first experience with macaroni and cheese was that familiar blue and orange box. I was in love with those neon orange noodles. Imagine my surprise when I learned that boxed mac and cheese was just the instant version of a real dish. It was mind-blowing to my five-year-old self. I took it upon myself to learn the secrets of macaroni, cheese and white sauce and ended up with the perfect combination of cheddar, Gruyère and Swiss.

INGREDIENTS

1 cup (110 g) _____ grated cheddar cheese

1 cup (100 g) _____ grated Gruyère cheese

1 cup (100 g) _____ grated Swiss cheese

1 ¾ cups (225 g) _____ macaroni

3 tbsp (45 g) _____ butter

¼ cup (35 g) _____ flour

2 ½ cups (600 ml) _____ milk

½ tsp _____ salt

½ tsp _____ pepper

1 tsp (2 g) _____ dry mustard

¼ tsp _____ smoked paprika

METHOD

Preheat the oven to 375°F (190°C).

Toss the three cheeses together in a bowl and mix well. Measure out 1 cup (105 g) and set aside for topping your mac and cheese.

Boil your macaroni until al dente, according the package. Ideally, start your sauce while the macaroni is cooking. When the macaroni is finished, drain, rinse with cold water and set aside until your sauce is finished.

In a medium sauce pan, over medium heat, melt the butter. Add the flour and stir constantly over medium heat for about 3 minutes, until smooth. Pour in 1 cup (240 ml) of the milk in a thin stream while whisking. When smooth, add the rest of the milk. Add the salt, pepper, dry mustard and smoked paprika. Keep on medium heat and stir for about 10 minutes, until the sauce thickens. Taste and adjust salt and pepper if needed.

Remove sauce from the heat and stir in 2 cups (210 g) of the cheese mixture. Stir until melted. Add the cheese sauce to the noodles and gently mix.

Pour the cheese and noodle into a 2-quart (2-l) ovenproof baking dish. Sprinkle on the remaining 1 cup (100 g) of cheese.

Bake for 25-30 minutes or until golden brown and crispy. Enjoy hot.

CLASSIC CARBONARA

SERVES: 2

BREAKFAST PASTA IN A BOWL

My first boss was a cute Italian woman who made it her mission to teach me about authentic Italian food. Once, she asked if I had ever tried carbonara. I'd never even heard of it, but she made it sound delicious: bacon, eggs, cheese and pasta. Breakfast food for dinner? Sold! I gave it a go that very night, but my "carbonara" didn't turn out anything like the pasta she described. Endless bowls of carbonara trials later and I've learned the secret: it's all about timing and a little bit of reserved pasta water.

INGREDIENTS

4 oz (115 g) _____ long pasta

¼ cup (30 g) _____ chopped pancetta

1 _____ large egg, room temp

¼ cup (28 g) _____ freshly grated parmesan

to taste _____ freshly ground pepper

½ tbsp (2 g) _____ chopped flat-leaf parsley

METHOD

Start by boiling a pot of water and cooking your pasta according to the package. Time it so that everything else is prepared by the time the pasta is cooked. Be sure to save ½ cup (120 ml) of pasta water when you drain the pasta.

Fry the pancetta in a large pan over medium heat until it starts to crisp at the edges, about 3-5 minutes.

In a large bowl, lightly beat the egg, then add the cheese, a liberal grinding of pepper and the chopped parsley. Mix thoroughly.

Add the cooked pasta to the pan and toss to coat each strand in the rendered fat. Pour the pasta and pancetta into the bowl with the egg and toss rapidly. If needed, add a bit of the hot pasta water a tablespoon (15 ml) at a time to help melt the cheese and cook the egg. Serve immediately.

CLASSIC

CARBONARA

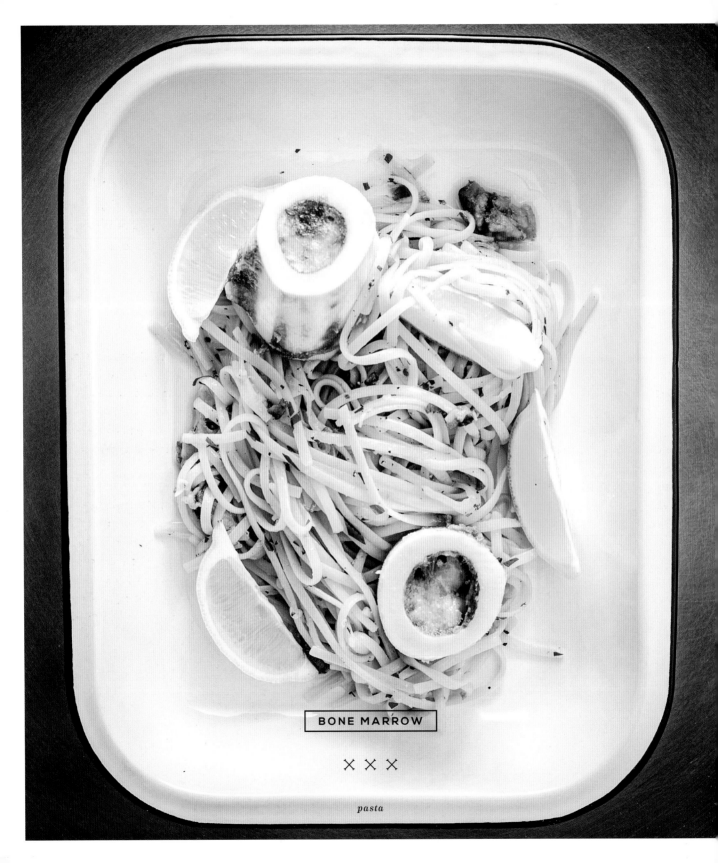

BONE MARROW

✕ ✕ ✕

pasta

BONE MARROW PASTA

SERVES: 2

ROASTED BEEF BONES, LEMON & PARMESAN TOSSED WITH LINGUINI

Bone marrow is rich, succulent and over-the-top. Sometimes, for a treat, I'll roast up some melty marrow bones to have with a toasted crunchy baguette. Once, a demi-baguette destined to be eaten with marrow went missing. It turned out that my husband, Mike, stole it to eat with pâté. I needed an emergency carb to go with the marrow, so I cooked up some pasta and tossed it all up with some lemon and parsley. It ended up being even better than the baguette.

INGREDIENTS

4-6 _____ bone marrow bones
4 oz (112 g) _____ linguini
1 tbsp (15 ml) _____ oil
1 _____ shallot, thinly sliced
zest _____ of 1 small lemon
2 tbsp (7.5 g) _____ chopped flat-leaf parsley
2 tbsp (11.25 g) _____ freshly grated parmesan
to taste _____ salt & freshly ground pepper
to serve _____ lemon wedges
if desired _____ crushed red pepper

METHOD

Preheat the oven to 450°F (230°C). Pat bones dry and place in a foil-lined roasting pan. Roast until marrow starts to loosen from the sides, 15-20 minutes. Marrow will start to drizzle out when it is done.

While the marrow is cooking, cook the pasta according to the package. Reserve ½ cup (120 ml) pasta water and drain. Set aside until marrow is cooked.

In a skillet, heat up the oil and sauté the shallots until soft. Add the pasta, lemon zest and flat-leaf parsley. When marrow is cooked, remove it from all but 2 of the bones using a small spoon or butter knife. Add the marrow and any fat that is on the roasting pan to the skillet. Add the parmesan and toss until pasta is coated. If dry, add 2 tablespoons (30 ml) of pasta water to loosen. Taste, season with salt and pepper and enjoy immediately with the remaining bone marrow bones, lemon wedges and red pepper flakes, if desired.

MIXED PAELLA

SERVES: 4-6

PRAWNS, CLAMS, CHICKEN, CHORIZO & SAFFRON RICE

Paella is one of those dishes that everyone has an opinion about. Even in Valencia, where paella comes from, different families will argue about what goes into a traditional paella. This paella is quite the opposite of traditional with its mix of meat and seafood, but it sure is delicious. Paella is an easy, low-maintenance, yet impressive crowd-pleasing dish. The smoky, saffron rice is so incredibly addictive that authentic or not, you'll fall in love.

INGREDIENTS

½ **tsp** _____ saffron threads

¼ **cup (60 ml)** _____ hot water

4 _____ chicken thighs, skin on

10-12 _____ large shrimp, peeled & deveined

to taste _____ salt & freshly ground pepper

¼ **cup (60 ml)** _____ oil

2 _____ fresh chorizos, removed from casings & crumbled

1 tbsp (6.8 g) _____ smoked paprika

3 _____ garlic cloves, minced

3 _____ tomatoes, finely diced

1 _____ small onion, diced

7 cups (1.7 l) _____ low-sodium chicken stock

2 ½ cups (500 g) _____ Valencia/Bomba rice

1 _____ red pepper, sliced into strips

12 _____ fresh clams

to serve _____ lemon wedges

METHOD

Put saffron in the hot water and let sit for 15 minutes. Season chicken and shrimp with salt and pepper. Heat oil in a 16-18 inch (40-45 cm) paella pan over medium-high heat. Add chicken, shrimp and chorizo and cook, turning occasionally, until browned, about 5-8 minutes. Transfer shrimp to a plate, leaving meats in pan. Add paprika, garlic, tomatoes and onions to pan and cook, stirring often, about 6 minutes. Add saffron mixture and stock, season with salt and bring to a boil over high heat.

Sprinkle in rice, distributing evenly with a spoon. Add peppers and cook, without stirring, until rice has absorbed most of the liquid, 12-15 minutes. Reduce heat to low, add shrimp and place clams in the rice hinge side down. Cook, without stirring, until clams have opened and rice has absorbed all of the liquid and is al dente, 5-10 minutes more. When rice is cooked, turn heat to high for 1-2 minutes to create crispy rice bits on the bottom. Remove pan from heat, cover with aluminum foil and let sit for 5 minutes before enjoying with lemon wedges.

MUSHROOM ORZO

SERVES: 2-4

CREAMY RISOTTO-STYLE ORZO

There's a tiny pintxo bar in San Sebastian, Spain that serves up some of the best food I've ever had. Everything I tasted was delicious, but one of the standouts was their take on risotto, made with orzo. I've never had orzo or risotto taste so creamy. They cook orzo the same way you would normally cook a risotto: the grains are toasted in oil and then cooked in stock. Orzo cooks a lot more quickly and easily than risotto as well, which makes it ideal for a weeknight dinner.

INGREDIENTS

3 tbsp (45 ml) _____ oil

1 _____ small onion, diced

2 cups (140 g) _____ sliced cremini mushrooms

1 cup (210 g) _____ orzo

2 cups plus ½ cup (595 ml) ___ vegetable stock

2 tbsp (11.25 g) _____ freshly grated parmesan

to taste _____ salt & freshly ground pepper

METHOD

Heat the oil in a large saucepan over medium heat. Add the onion and sauté until translucent, but not brown. Add the mushrooms and sauté until deeply brown and caramelized. Add the orzo and stir to coat and lightly toast, about 2 minutes.

Add 2 cups (475 ml) of stock and bring to a boil over high heat, then reduce heat and simmer, stirring every so often, until orzo is tender to bite and most of the liquid is absorbed, about 10-12 minutes. Remove from the heat, stir in the parmesan, season to taste with salt and pepper and serve immediately.

Note: If mixture becomes too thick before the orzo is done, add a little more stock, ¼ cup (60 ml) at a time.

TOMATO BASIL SPAGHETTI

SERVES: 4-6

FRESH TOMATO SAUCE, CREAMY BURRATA, PEPPERY BASIL

Simple is best. It rarely gets more delicious than a plate of perfectly cooked pasta, fresh tomatoes, basil and cheese. But simple doesn't mean boring or plain, especially if you're using burrata. Burrata is a fresh cheese with a thin mozzarella shell and a creamy, dreamy, meltingly soft center. It's fantastic with just a drizzle of olive oil and salt and pepper, but resist if you can, and toss it with spaghetti, basil and tomatoes.

INGREDIENTS

16 oz (450 g) _____ spaghetti

10 oz (280 g) _____ cherry tomatoes

1 tbsp (15 ml) _____ oil

3 _____ garlic cloves, minced

1 tsp (2 g) _____ crushed red pepper

10-12 leaves _____ fresh basil, torn

to taste _____ salt & freshly ground pepper

2 balls burrata, torn into 1-inch (2.5-cm) pieces

METHOD

Cook the pasta according to the package.

Slice the tomatoes in half. Place in a bowl, making sure to save the juices.

Heat up the oil in a large skillet over medium heat. Add the tomatoes, garlic and crushed red pepper and cook, stirring often until the tomatoes are soft, 5-6 minutes. Press down on the tomatoes to release their juices. Simmer on low to medium-low until sauce is thick, about 8-9 minutes. Remove the pan from the heat and set aside.

When the pasta is cooked, reserve 1 cup (240 ml) of pasta cooking water and drain pasta.

Add the pasta to the skillet with the tomatoes and turn the heat to medium. Toss the pasta so the sauce coats each strand of pasta. If the sauce is too thick or dry, add a small amount of pasta water until the desired consistency has been achieved. Add half of the torn basil and season with salt and pepper to taste. Serve immediately with the torn burrata and remaining basil sprinkled on top.

TOMATO
BASIL
SPAGHETTI

FAST & FRESH

EASY & DELICIOUS

Lasanga
W/ BÉCHAMEL
& BOLOGNESE

LASAGNA W/BÉCHAMEL & BOLOGNESE

SERVES: 6-8

FIVE LAYERS OF BÉCHAMEL, RAGÙ, NOODLES & CHEESE

I remember stealing my brother's Garfield comics and hiding under my bed with a flashlight to read them when I was little. I thought Garfield was the epitome of funny and I loved his obsession with lasagna, which was my brother's obsession too. My mom would make a huge tray at the beginning of the week and he'd have a slice as a snack every day. My lasagna is nothing like my mom's, but my brother (who is an expert in these things) has told me secretly that it's better.

INGREDIENTS

2 tbsp (30 ml) _____ oil, divided

2 _____ onions, diced

4 _____ carrots, diced

4 _____ celery stalks, diced

4 _____ garlic cloves, minced

2 tsp (4 g) _____ crushed red pepper

1 lb (450 g) _____ ground beef

1 lb (450 g) _____ ground pork

4 cups (960 ml) _____ beef stock

½ cup (120 ml) _____ tomato paste

4 _____ bay leaves

4 _____ sprigs fresh thyme

to taste _____ salt & freshly ground pepper

¼ cup (57 g) _____ butter

¼ cup (35 g) _____ all-purpose flour

2 ½ cups (600 ml) _____ milk

pinch _____ nutmeg

pinch _____ cayenne

to taste _____ salt & freshly ground pepper

15 _____ cooked lasanga noodles

2 cups (224 g) _____ shredded mozzarella

¼ cup (22.5 g) _____ freshly grated parmesan

METHOD

In a large stockpot, heat 1 tablespoon (15 ml) oil over medium-high heat. Add the onions, carrots and celery. Deeply brown, about 15 minutes. Remove from the pot and set aside. In the same pot, heat up the remaining oil over medium heat. Add the garlic and crushed red pepper and cook for 2 minutes. Add the meats and brown over medium-high, about 15 minutes. Add the vegetables, stock, tomato paste, bay leaves and thyme. Bring to a boil and lower to a bare simmer for 1-2 hours. If the water level gets low, add water 2 tablespoons (30 ml) at a time. When finished, discard thyme and bay leaves, taste and season with salt and pepper.

Preheat the oven to 400°F (205°C). Make the béchamel: over medium heat, melt the butter. Add the flour and stir constantly over medium heat for 3 minutes, until smooth. Pour in 1 cup (240 ml) of the milk in a thin stream while whisking. When smooth, add the rest of the milk. Keep on medium heat and whisk for about 10 minutes, until the sauce thickens. Add the nutmeg and cayenne. Taste and season with salt and pepper.

In an 8x11-inch (20x28-cm) baking dish, spread out ½ cup (120 ml) of ragù. Add a layer of noodles, and then evenly spread out 1 cup ragù (240 ml), ¼ cup (60 ml) béchamel and ⅓ cup (35 g) mozzarella. Repeat 4 times until you have 5 layers of pasta. On the final layer, sprinkle on all of the remaining mozzarella and add the parmesan.

Bake for 40-45 minutes, until bubbly and brown. Let rest for 10 minutes and serve.

·ASIAN-STYLE·

Pasta

SPICY & SEASONED WITH SOY!

HOME-STYLE ASIAN PASTA

SERVES: 3-4

MINCED BEEF & PORK WITH SOY SAUCE & CRUSHED RED PEPPER

Often the best recipes come from making do with what you have in the fridge. You can get pretty creative when you're hungry in the middle of the night and nothing is open, not even late-night pizza delivery. This happens to me and Mike more often than not. One night, the two of us collaborated on this pasta dish, deciding to give it a double dose of savory umami flavor using soy sauce and tomato paste. This sauce is hearty, spicy and perfect when you want a quick pasta dish with a twist.

INGREDIENTS

2 tbsp (30 ml) _____ oil
1 _____ carrot, diced
1 _____ onion, diced
2 _____ garlic cloves, finely minced
2 tsp (4 g) _____ crushed red pepper
1 tbsp (15 ml) _____ oil

2 tbsp (30 ml) _____ oil
¼ lb (112 g) _____ ground beef
¼ lb (112 g) _____ ground pork
1 tsp (5 ml) _____ soy sauce
2 tbsp (30 ml) _____ cream
1 cup (240 ml) _____ beef stock
½ cup (120 ml) _____ tomato paste

8 oz (225 g) _____ short pasta

METHOD

Heat oil in a small pot over medium heat and add the carrots, onions, garlic and pepper flakes. Stir and cook the mixture over medium to medium-low heat, until very soft and tender, about 15-20 minutes.

In a skillet, heat the oil over medium-high and brown the meat thoroughly. Stir in the soy sauce then add the cream, beef stock and tomato paste. Bring the mixture to a boil and then turn down the heat until just simmering. When the liquid is about 80% gone, add the cooked vegetables and mix well. Taste and season accordingly. Keep the sauce warm while you cook your pasta.

Cook your pasta according to the package instructions. Toss the hot pasta in the sauce and enjoy immediately with extra crushed red pepper on top.

SEAFOOD PAPPARDELLE

SERVES: 4

SCALLOPS, SHRIMP & PASTA IN SPICY TOMATO-CREAM SAUCE

The first time I tried rose sauce at a restaurant, I was obsessed. I had never heard of it before, but one taste of that silky, creamy, tomatoey sauce, and I was hooked. I asked the waiter if he knew how the kitchen made it and he said it was basically just tomato sauce and cream. This is a spicy, extra-creamy version of a basic rose. The grilled seafood takes this pasta dish over the top, but if you like, you can always substitute in grilled chicken or vegetables instead.

INGREDIENTS

1 tbsp (15 ml) _____ oil
1 tbsp (15 g) _____ butter
1 lb (450 g) _____ scallops
1 lb (450 g) _____ shrimp, peeled & deveined
2 _____ garlic cloves, minced
½ tsp _____ crushed red pepper
1 ½ cups (360 ml) _____ basic tomato sauce
(page 40)
¼ cup (60 ml) _____ heavy cream
8 oz (225 g) _____ pappardelle
to serve _____ chopped flat-leaf parsley

METHOD

In a large skillet, heat up the oil and butter over medium to medium-high heat. Sear the scallops and shrimp, about 1 minute per side. Remove from the pan and set aside. Turn the heat to medium and add the garlic and pepper flakes. Cook until soft, but not brown. Add the tomato sauce and cream. Return the scallops and shrimp to the pan and simmer gently on low while the pasta is cooking.

Cook the pappardelle according to the package. Drain and toss with the sauce and seafood. Enjoy immediately with a sprinkling of flat-leaf parsley.

SEAFOOD
PAPPARDELLE

SESAME
NOODLE
SALAD

SESAME
NOODLE SALAD

SERVES: 4-6

CRISP VEGETABLES, CHICKEN & NOODLES IN VINEGAR-SESAME DRESSING

I once threw an all-you-can-eat Chinese buffet-themed dinner party where the star was supposed to be homemade dumplings. This noodle salad ending up stealing the show, though. The party had barely started and I had only turned my back on the giant bowl of noodles for a few seconds, but the next thing I knew, friends were coming up to me asking if there was more noodle salad. Sadly, my all-you-can-eat buffet party didn't actually end up being all-you-can-eat, but at least I knew I had a keeper.

INGREDIENTS

⅓ cup (80 ml) _____ rice vinegar
⅓ cup (80 ml) _____ oil
2 tbsp (30 ml) _____ sriracha
1 tbsp (15 ml) _____ sesame oil
8 oz (225 g) _____ egg/mung bean noodles
2 cups (300 g) _____ poached chicken breast,
shredded (page 196)
4 cups (188 g) _____ shredded romaine
1 cup (92 g) _____ sliced bell peppers
1 cup (120 g) _____ julienned cucumbers
1 cup (100 g) _____ sliced celery
1 cup (40 g) _____ roughly chopped cilantro
3 _____ green onions, sliced
to taste _____ salt & freshly ground pepper
1 tbsp (9 g) _____ sesame seeds

METHOD

In a large bowl, whisk together the rice vinegar, oil, sriracha and sesame oil. Add the noodles, chicken breast, romaine, peppers, cucumber, celery, cilantro and green onions. Toss until everything is evenly dressed. Taste, season with salt and pepper and enjoy immediately or chilled with sesame seeds.

SCALLOP FRIED RICE

SERVES: 2

CRISPY RICE WITH SCALLOPS, EGG WHITES & BROCCOLINI

Fried rice is my go-to meal when I'm in a hurry and want something fast, easy and delicious. Generally, fried rice is made with whatever's in the fridge, but here it gets a bit fancier with tender scallops and crisp broccolini. Cold day-old rice that's had a chance to lose its moisture is best for caramelization and crispness. If you have to use freshly cooked rice, try to cool it off as much as you can before frying it otherwise you'll end up with a soggy mess.

INGREDIENTS

as needed	oil
7 oz (200 g)	small scallops
2	large egg whites
2 cups (320 g)	cold, cooked rice
1 cup (91 g)	broccolini, sliced
⅓ cup (28 g)	sliced green onion
to taste	salt & freshly ground pepper
2 tbsp (30 ml)	oil
4	garlic cloves, minced

METHOD

In a wok or large sauté pan, add enough oil to lightly coat the bottom of a wok or large sauté pan. Heat the oil on medium. When the oil is hot, add the scallops and cook, about 1 minute per side. Remove from the pan and set aside.

Add more oil to the pan if needed and scramble the egg whites until almost set. Remove from the pan and set aside.

Add a bit more oil to the pan and heat over medium-high heat. Add the rice and fry until warmed through and slightly crispy. Stir in the egg whites, scallops, broccolini and green onions, and continue to fry until all the ingredients are mixed well. Taste and season with salt and pepper.

To make the crispy garlic, heat up oil over medium-low heat in a small nonstick skillet. Add garlic and fry until golden and crisp, stirring occasionally, about 1-2 minutes. Remove from the oil and drain on paper towels. Sprinkle on the fried rice. You will have extra garlic crisps, which taste fantastic on sunny-side up eggs.

SCALLOP FRIED RICE

LEMONGRASS PORK & NOODLES

SERVES: 4

VIETNAMESE GRILLED PORK WITH VERMICELLI, PICKLES & FISH SAUCE

One of the best things to eat in the summer is Vietnamese bun: hot charred meat, cold noodles, lettuce, pickles and fresh herbs drenched in a salty-sweet fish sauce vinaigrette. The range of temperatures and contrast in textures are delicious on warm afternoons. This lemongrass marinade works well on all meats, not just pork, so feel free to use your preferred protein. No matter what, you'll end up with a light, refreshingly addictive bowl.

INGREDIENTS

1 lb (453 g) _____ pork butt/shoulder

2 tsp (13 g) _____ minced lemongrass
2 _____ garlic cloves, minced
2 tsp (8 g) _____ sugar
1 _____ small shallot, finely minced
1 tbsp (15 ml) _____ oil
1 tbsp (15 ml) _____ fish sauce
½ tsp _____ freshly ground pepper

1 _____ large carrot, julienned
2" (5 cm) _____ piece of daikon, julienned
½ tsp _____ salt
2 tsp (10 g) _____ sugar

16 oz (500 g) _____ package of vermicelli

to taste _____ fresh mint leaves
to taste _____ Thai basil
to taste _____ shiso leaves
to taste _____ cilantro
to taste _____ bean sprouts
to taste _____ sliced cucumbers
to serve _____ fish sauce vinaigrette (page 196)

METHOD

Slice the pork as thinly as possible. Thoroughly mix the pork slices with the lemongrass, garlic, sugar, shallot, oil, fish sauce and ground pepper. Marinate for 1-2 hours.

Make the pickles: put the carrots and daikon into a bowl and sprinkle on the salt and sugar. After 15 minutes, rinse off the pickles and place in the fridge until ready to assemble bowls.

Grill or pan fry the pork over medium-high heat until slightly charred and cooked through, about 1-2 minutes per side.

Cook vermicelli according to the package instructions. Rinse in cold water.

To assemble, divide the vermicelli into 4 bowls. Top equally with grilled meat, pickles and garnish. Serve with fish sauce vinaigrette on the side; pour on top of noodles and meat to taste.

GRILLED *Lemongrass* PORK WITH VERMICELLI

MEATS

I am an unabashed meat lover. I love the way it tastes and how it can elevate a simple meal into an elegant one. I love meat so much that at fifteen, when I announced that I was going to be a vegetarian, my mom laughed in my face. I spent the next three months eating boiled vegetables because my mom refused to cook anything without meat. She was convinced that my inability to cook would cause me to cave and go back to my meat-eating ways. She was right.

Three months of not having my mom as my personal short order cook made me realize that I needed to learn how to cook for myself. She probably had no idea that she was creating an obsessed cooking monster, but I like to think that it was a bonus (aside from the astronomically high grocery bills).

The best thing about most meat recipes is that they're slow and hands off. Just prepare your meat a day in advance, slow cook it the next day and you'll have delicious meaty goodness like crispy Porchetta and classic Braised Beef Brisket. With these recipes in your pocket, you'll never be as hungry as I was at fifteen.

STEAK
& BUTTER

SERVES: 2

BUTTER-BASTED RIB EYE WITH SHALLOTS, GARLIC & THYME

A perfectly cooked medium-rare steak is beautiful: crusty, deep brown char gives way to pleasantly rosy pink juicy insides. Steak is one of those things that everyone takes pride in mastering, but few really agree on how to properly cook. Butter basting your steak is a standard restaurant trick that will take it over the top. Butter, infused with shallots, garlic and thyme, adds another layer of flavor to an already delicious piece of meat.

INGREDIENTS

2-2 ½ lbs (900-1125g) _____ thick rib-eye steak, at least 1 ½-inch (3.8-cm) thick

as needed _____ kosher salt

as needed _____ freshly ground pepper

¼ cup (57 g) _____ butter, room temp

3 _____ garlic cloves, peeled & crushed

1 _____ medium shallot, sliced

4 _____ fresh thyme sprigs

METHOD

Pat the steak dry with paper towels and season liberally with salt and pepper. Let rest at room temperature for 45 minutes.

Heat a cast-iron pan over high heat for 3 minutes, until it just begins to smoke. When the pan is hot, add the steak. After 2 minutes, flip the steak using a pair of tongs. Sear the opposite side for 2 minutes and then flip back to the first side.

Reduce the heat to medium-low and immediately add the butter, garlic, sliced shallots and thyme. If the butter starts to smoke excessively, remove the pan from the heat for a minute. When the butter is bubbling, baste the steak: tilt the pan so the butter pools, scoop it up with a large spoon and pour over the steak, making sure to aim at any light-colored spots. Baste for 4 minutes, then flip and baste the other side for 1-2 minutes. The steak should be a deep mahogany brown. Use a meat thermometer to check the internal temperature: 120-125°F (49-52°C) for rare. If you prefer medium-rare, continue basting for another two minutes on each side or until the internal temperature reads 130-135°F (54-57°C).

Transfer the steak to a plate, keeping the butter in the pan, and let rest for 8 minutes (the steak will continue to cook while resting). To serve, cut the steak off the bone and slice against the grain into ½-inch (1.3-cm) slabs. Arrange on a plate and drizzle with the reserved butter.

PORCHETTA

SERVES: 6-8

SLOW-ROASTED PORK BELLY WRAPPED LOIN

Porchetta is an Italian boneless pork roast that has the most addictive flavors and contrast of textures. Traditionally, porchetta is a whole pig that has been deboned, herbed, rolled back together and slow roasted. This minified version uses tenderloin and skin-on pork belly. The best part of porchetta is that after a bit of prep work, you get to sit back, relax and let the oven do its work. After four hours of roasting you'll have crispy, crunchy, juicy pork perfection.

INGREDIENTS

1 tbsp (10 g) _____ kosher salt

2 tsp (0.6 g) _____ fresh rosemary, chopped

2 tsp (4 g) _____ fennel seed, crushed

2 tsp (4 g) _____ crushed red pepper

2 tsp (4 g) _____ freshly ground pepper

zest _____ of 1 lemon

2 tbsp (7.5 g) _____ roughly chopped
flat-leaf parsley

2 tbsp (2 g) _____ fresh rosemary

1-2 lbs (450-900 g) ____ small pork tenderloin,
around 3-inch (7.5-cm) in diameter

12-inch (30-cm) 3 lbs (1.35 kg) _ skin-on pork belly

as needed _____ oil

as needed _____ string

METHOD

Combine the salt, rosemary, fennel seed, crushed red pepper, pepper and lemon zest in a small bowl. In another small bowl, mix together the flat-leaf parsley and rosemary. Place the belly skin-side down on a cutting board and lightly score the meat. Sprinkle on half of the salt mix. Spread out the herb mix on top of the salt and place the tenderloin in the center of the belly. Tightly roll the belly around the tenderloin and tie together with kitchen twine. Rub the skin generously with oil and the remaining salt mix. Tightly wrap the porchetta in plastic wrap, place in a dish and put in the fridge overnight.

The next day, heat the oven to 275°F (135°C). Unwrap the porchetta, pat dry with paper towels and place on a rack in a deep roasting pan. Roast on the center rack of the oven for 4 hours. Use a meat thermometer to check that the internal temperature is 145°F (63°C). Blast the heat up to 450°F (235°C) and continue to roast for 20-25 minutes, keeping an eye on the skin. You want the skin crackling golden brown and crispy.

Remove from the oven, let rest for 15-20 minutes, slice and enjoy!

GRILLED FLANK STEAK

SERVES: 4-6

SOY SAUCE & HONEY-MARINATED FLANK

My mother-in-law is excellent at creating marinades for meat. I'll taste something that she's made, ask her for the recipe and inevitably, she'll tell me it's just soy sauce and sugar, when it's obviously so much more. I've done my fair share of tasting and experimenting and this is my take on her sweet and savory marinade. The honey creates a deep-brown caramelized crust and the rice vinegar adds a gentle tang.

INGREDIENTS

¼ **cup (60 ml)** _____ oil

4 _____ garlic cloves, minced

2 tbsp (30 ml) _____ rice vinegar

¼ **cup (60 ml)** _____ soy sauce

2 tbsp (30 ml) _____ honey

2 tbsp (12 g) _____ finely minced ginger

½ **cup (42 g)** _____ sliced green onions

2 lb (900 g) _____ flank steak

to serve _____ roasted sesame oil

to serve _____ sliced green onions

METHOD

Mix together the oil, garlic, rice vinegar, soy sauce, honey, ginger and green onions in a large, shallow container. Add the flank steak and marinate overnight.

When ready to cook, remove the steak from the marinade, brushing off any stuck-on bits. Grill or pan fry the streak.

To pan fry: Heat up a large heavy cast-iron pan over high heat. Add 2 tablespoons (30 ml) of oil and when shimmery, add the steak. Sear for 3 minutes and flip, searing for another 3 minutes. Remove the pan from the heat and let the residual heat cook the steak to your preference, 125°F (52°C) for rare and 130° (55°C) for medium rare. Remove the steak from the pan, set on a cutting board and rest for 10 minutes, covered with foil.

To grill: Preheat one side of your grill to high. Do not heat the other side. Oil the grill and place the steak on the hot side, close the lid and grill until charred, about 3 minutes per side, until the internal temperature is 125°F (52°C) for rare and 130° (55°C) for medium rare. Remove the steak from the grill, set on a cutting board and rest for 10 minutes, covered with foil.

Cut the steak in thin slices, at an angle, against the grain. Serve with a drizzle of roasted sesame oil and sliced green onions.

BRAISED BEEF BRISKET

SERVES: 4-6

A CLASSIC ROSEMARY & THYME POT ROAST

There's something comforting about a braise in the oven. It fills the house with delicious smells and makes every corner feel like home. This is easy, hands-off gourmet cooking at its best. Just a little bit of searing at the start of the dish and you'll have the afternoon free to do as you please. When you're ready to eat, it'll be a simple meal of meat and potatoes in their most delicious incarnation: fork-tender brisket and creamy new potatoes.

INGREDIENTS

1 tbsp (15 ml) _____ oil

2 lbs (900 g) _____ beef brisket, trimmed

1 _____ onion, sliced

3 _____ shallots, sliced

4 _____ garlic cloves, minced

4 _____ carrots, cut in 1-inch (2.5-cm) pieces

4 _____ celery, cut in 1-inch (2.5-cm) pieces

1 _____ sprig thyme

1 _____ sprig rosemary

3 _____ bay leaves

2 cups (480 ml) _____ beef stock

1 lb (450 g) _____ new potatoes, if desired

METHOD

Preheat the oven to 350°F (180°C).

In a large ovenproof pot, heat up the oil over medium-high to high heat. Sear the brisket, about 5 minutes per side. Remove and set aside.

If the pot is dry, add a bit of oil. Cook the onions and shallots over medium heat until soft and translucent. Add the garlic, carrots and celery and cook, about 8 minutes. Add the seared meat, thyme, rosemary, bay leaves and stock. Bring to a boil, cover and place in the oven for 3-3 ½ hours. If using potatoes, add them to the pot 2 hours after you place the brisket in the oven.

To serve, remove the brisket from the liquid and slice against the grain. Serve with the cooking liquid.

GARLIC THYME CHOPS

SERVES: 2

PAN-ROASTED, BUTTER-BASTED THICK-CUT PORK CHOPS

I grew up eating pork chops and never really liking them, but, then again, the pork chops of my childhood were nothing like these foolproof juicy, thick-cut, on-the-bone beauties. As with most meats, brining overnight helps the chops develop flavor and retain moistness. Their thickness will make them hard to overcook and basting with garlic and thyme butter adds that extra boost of complexity and deliciousness.

INGREDIENTS

2 cups (480 ml) _____ apple cider

1 cup (240 ml) _____ hot water

1 tbsp (24 g) _____ salt

¼ cup (50 g) _____ sugar

2 tsp (6 g) _____ mustard powder

2-inch (5-cm) 1 ¼ lb (560g) _ bone-in pork chop

1 tbsp (15 ml) _____ oil

2 tbsp (30 g) _____ butter

2 _____ garlic cloves, crushed

3 _____ sprigs fresh thyme

METHOD

In a container with a cover, stir together the apple cider, hot water, salt, sugar and mustard powder until the salt and sugar dissolves. Chill in the fridge. When cold, place pork chop in brine, making sure it is submerged. Brine overnight in the fridge.

Preheat the oven to 400°F (205°C). Rinse off the pork chop and pat dry.

In a cast-iron skillet or stainless steel heavy-bottomed pan, heat up oil over medium-high heat. Sear chop until dark golden brown, about 4 minutes per side.

Place the skillet in the oven and roast for 10 minutes, flipping at the 5 minute mark.

Place the skillet on the stove top and turn the heat to medium-low. Add the butter, garlic and thyme and baste for 2 minutes, then flip and baste for another 2 minutes. Check to make sure the internal temperature is 145°F (63°C). If lower, baste for several more minutes until it comes up to 145°F (63°C).

Rest the chop for 15 minutes, slice and enjoy.

GARLIC-THYME

CHOPS

THICK AND JUICY

PORK BELLY

SERVES: 3-4

SWEET & SAVORY SLOW-ROASTED PORK

Roast pork belly is one of those dishes that immediately impresses as it comes out of the oven — the hunk of glossy, juicy meat just begs you to slice into it. What I like best about this recipe is that, with a little planning ahead, it's basically hands off. All you need to do is marinate your roast the night before and pop it in the oven for a slow roast the next day. The result is an easy, meltingly soft, decadent piece of meat with a subtle hint of spice.

INGREDIENTS

1 tbsp (9 g) _____ kosher salt

2 tbsp (30 g) _____ sugar

2 tbsp (30 ml) _ sambal oelek (chili garlic sauce)

1 ½ lbs (680 g) _____ pork belly, skin off

METHOD

In a small bowl, mix together the salt, sugar and sambal. Rub the marinade evenly on the pork. Place the belly in a snug container and refrigerate covered overnight.

The next day, preheat the oven to 250°F (120°C). Wipe off any excess marinade and place belly in a roasting tray. Roast for 3 hours, until tender and cooked through. Turn the oven up to 400°F (205°C) to give the belly some color, 15-20 minutes. Let rest for 15 minutes, slice into ½-inch (1.3-cm) slices and enjoy immediately.

·PAN-ROASTED·
·CHICKEN THIGHS·

PAN-ROASTED CHICKEN THIGHS

SERVES: 2-4

SLOW-COOKED CRISPY THIGHS WITH THYME & LEMON

Slow cooking chicken thighs over low heat will create the crispiest, juiciest thighs you've ever tasted. Like most of the meat recipes so far, this recipe is pretty hands off, so if, like me, you're not inclined to stand next to the stove while they're cooking, just make sure to check in every so often to make sure the skin isn't browning too quickly. If you have one, a splatter screen is pretty handy for keeping your stovetop clean, but don't use a regular lid or the chicken skin won't be as crispy.

INGREDIENTS

4-6 _____ skin on, bone-in chicken thighs

as needed _____ salt & freshly ground pepper

1 tbsp (15 ml) _____ oil

4-6 _____ fresh thyme sprigs

to serve _____ lemon wedges

METHOD

Pat the chicken thighs dry with paper towels. Season with salt and pepper. Heat oil in a large, deep skillet over medium-high heat. Add the chicken thighs, being sure not to crowd, skin-side down and sear for 2 minutes. Turn the heat down to medium-low to low and cook for 25-30 minutes until the skin is crispy and golden brown and most of the fat is rendered out. Keep an eye on the chicken; if it starts to brown too quickly, turn the heat down as low as it will go.

Flip the chicken skin-side up and cook for 10 more minutes. Add the thyme to the rendered fat. Check to see if chicken is cooked through: the meat should be opaque and there should be no pink near the bone. Remove from the pan and rest for 5 minutes. Serve with lemon wedges.

BUTTERMILK FRIED CHICKEN

SERVES: 4-6

DOUBLE-COATED DRUMSTICKS & THIGHS

Hot, crispy, deep-fried chicken skin and juicy meat is one of life's greatest food pleasures. If you've never deep fried before, be warned: once you start, you'll be addicted. Deep frying is actually pretty easy, as long as you have the right tools and everything set up beforehand. Some key advice for fantastic fried chicken: use a thermometer to monitor your oil, make sure your oil has a high smoking point (like grape seed or rice bran) and make sure you're deep frying in a high-sided pot to avoid any spillage.

INGREDIENTS

8 _____ chicken drumsticks and thighs

1 ½ cups (360 ml) _____ buttermilk
1 tsp (8 g) _____ salt
1 tsp (2 g) _____ pepper

3 cups (420 g) _____ all-purpose flour
1 tbsp (9 g) _____ garlic powder
1 tbsp (9 g) _____ onion powder
2 tsp (4 g) _____ paprika
2 tsp (4 g) _____ cayenne
2 tsp (6 g) _____ salt
2 tsp (4 g) _____ pepper

as needed _____ grape seed or rice bran oil

METHOD

One hour before frying your chicken, remove it from the fridge and let it come to room temperature.

Whisk together the buttermilk, salt and pepper in a large bowl. In another large bowl, mix together the coating: flour, garlic powder, onion powder, paprika, cayenne, salt and pepper. Transfer half of the flour mix to a third bowl. Set up a dipping station: coating, buttermilk, coating. Two bowls of coating helps avoid large lumps.

Dip the chicken in the first bowl of coating, then the buttermilk and finally in the second bowl of coating. Place your double-coated pieces of chicken on a plate or baking sheet while heating up the oil.

In a deep-sided pot, add 2-3 inches (5-7.5 cm) of oil. Heat over medium heat until the oil is 350°F (180°C). Carefully lower 2-3 pieces of chicken into the oil. The temperature of the oil will drop, so adjust the heat to maintain 300-325°F (150-160°C). Fry for 12-14 minutes, flipping every so often, until the chicken is a deep golden brown. Remove the chicken and check to see if chicken is cooked through: the meat should be opaque and there should be no pink near the bone. Drain fried chicken on a wire rack in a pan. Repeat until all pieces are fried. Let rest for 5 minutes then serve.

BUTTERMILK FRIED **CHICKEN**

SWEET **&** SPICY
CHICKEN

SWEET & SPICY CHICKEN

SERVES: 4

VIETNAMESE PAN-FRIED CHICKEN WITH FISH SAUCE

Fish sauce, if you're not familiar with it, is a salty, golden brown sauce made from fermented fish. It doesn't sound all that appealing, but it adds a depth of flavor that can't be substituted. Luckily, it's pretty easy to find these days and I guarantee you'll find lots of uses for it. Here, fish sauce combines with sugar, chili and lime to create a deliciously sweet and spicy caramel coating. This chicken is great on it's own, but even better with rice for soaking up the sauce.

INGREDIENTS

6 _____ boneless, skinless chicken thighs

3 tbsp (45 ml) _____ oil, divided

3 _____ garlic cloves, minced

¼ cup (60 ml) _____ water

3 tbsp (45 g) _____ sugar

3 tbsp (45 ml) _____ fish sauce

juice _____ of ½ lime

1 _____ Thai chili, thinly sliced

¼ cup (10 g) _____ chopped mint & cilantro

METHOD

Cut the thighs into 1-inch (2.5-cm) pieces. Heat up a large nonstick pan over medium-high heat and add 1 tablespoon (15 ml) oil. When hot and shimmery, add the thigh pieces and cook, stirring every so often, until the chicken is cooked through, 12-15 minutes.

While the chicken is cooking, make the crispy garlic bits. Heat up 2 tablespoons (30 ml) of oil over medium-low heat in a small nonstick skillet. Add the minced garlic and fry until golden and crisp, stirring occasionally, about 1-2 minutes. Remove from the oil and drain on paper towels.

Once the chicken is cooked through, add the water, sugar, fish sauce, lime juice and Thai chili. Stir, then bring to a boil and reduce the sauce over high heat until glossy and sticky. Garnish with garlic bits, mint and cilantro. Enjoy immediately.

PULLED PORK

SERVES: 4-6

SLOW-ROASTED PORK SHOULDER

Pulled pork is perfect for those times when you don't feel like working very hard, but want to dig into something meaty and savory. All you have to do is rub a pork shoulder with salt, sugar and a bit of sambal oelek (or other hot sauce) and let it sit overnight in the fridge. The next day, pop it into a low-temperature oven and wait for the magic to happen. Cooking low and slow breaks the meat down into easy-to-pull-apart pieces, ideal for filling sandwiches, tacos or eating with your favorite carbs.

INGREDIENTS

1 tbsp (9 g) _____ kosher salt
2 tbsp (30 g) _____ sugar
2 tbsp (30 ml) ___ sambal oelek/thick hot sauce
3 lbs (1.35 kg) _____ boneless pork shoulder

METHOD

Mix together the salt, sugar and sambal oelek and rub all over the meat. Place in a large bowl, cover and put in the fridge for at least 6 hours, but no more than 24.

Preheat the oven to 250°F (120°C). Rinse off the pork and place in a roasting pan. Roast for 4 hours, basting with the rendered fat and pan juices every hour. Remove from the oven and rest for 30 minutes.

Use two forks to pull apart the meat and enjoy immediately.

PULLED
PORK
SLOW ROASTED

MAPLE GLAZED DUCK

MAPLE-GLAZED DUCK

SERVES: 2

CRISPY DUCK WITH MAPLE BOURBON SAUCE & HONEY SRIRACHA CARROTS

Duck was always a special treat when I was a kid. It also happened to be my dad's favorite food, so it was a treat we had quite often — although me and my brother had to fight my dad to get a taste. I've heard that when he was young, my dad ate whole roasted ducks by himself and I'm not surprised. Duck is delicious, especially when it has extra crispy skin and is served with maple bourbon sauce and honey sriracha carrots.

INGREDIENTS

2 (10 oz [280 g]) _____ duck breasts

as needed _____ salt & freshly ground pepper

4 cups (420 g) _____ chopped carrots, about 4-5 carrots

1 tbsp (15 g) _____ butter

2 tsp (10 ml) _____ honey

4 tsp (20 ml) _____ sriracha

2 tbsp (30 ml) _____ duck fat

1 tbsp (10 g) _____ all-purpose flour

2 tbsp (30 ml) _____ bourbon

2 tbsp (30 ml) _____ maple syrup

¼ cup (60 ml) _____ chicken stock

1 tsp (5 ml) _____ sriracha

as needed _____ salt & freshly ground pepper

METHOD

Preheat your oven to 425°F (220°C). Lightly score the duck skin and season with salt and pepper. Put the carrots in a stockpot and cover with water. Bring to a boil and then reduce and simmer until carrots are very tender, 15-20 minutes.

While the carrots are simmering, cook the breasts skin-side down without oil in a nonstick pan, on medium heat, for 6 to 8 minutes or until a deep golden brown. Flip and sear the other side of each breast for 30 seconds to 1 minute. Move the breasts skin-side down onto a roasting tray. Place in the middle of the oven and cook for 10 minutes for medium-rare and up to 20 minutes for well-done. Remove the duck from the pan and rest, skin-side up for 5 minutes. Reserve the duck fat for the sauce.

While the duck is resting, make the sauce. In a small saucepan, heat the duck fat over medium heat. Add the flour and stir until smooth and incorporated. Add the bourbon, maple syrup, stock and sriracha. Continue to stir over medium heat until the sauce starts to thicken. Taste and adjust salt and pepper if needed.

By this point, the carrots should be tender. Blend the carrots until smooth. Push through a fine mesh sieve, and then stir in the butter, honey and sriracha.

Slice the duck into 1-inch (2.5-cm) pieces and enjoy with maple bourbon sauce and honeyed sriracha carrots.

CURRY CHICKEN POT PIE

SERVES: 4-6

A CREAMY, CURRIED TAKE ON A CLASSIC

Certain foods remind me of certain seasons. Chicken pot pie belongs to fall. Crispy, cold air, crunchy leaves and quickly darkening evenings are the best time for curling up with a steaming chicken pot pie. This version mixes it up a bit with curry and coconut. It's a bit different but still creamy and comfortingly full of chicken, potatoes and carrots. If you're not a fan of puff pastry, you can definitely eat this as a curry chicken stew.

INGREDIENTS

1 ½ lbs (675 g) _____ boneless, skinless chicken thighs, cut into 1-inch (2.5-cm) pieces

2 tbsp (12 g) _____ Madras curry powder

2 tsp (10 ml) _ sambal oelek (chili garlic sauce)

½ tsp _____ freshly ground pepper

1 _____ medium shallot, minced

2 _____ garlic cloves, minced

1 tbsp (20 g) _____ finely minced lemongrass

1 tbsp (15 ml) _____ oil

1 _____ large russet potato peeled & cut into 1-inch (2.5-cm) pieces

2 _____ large carrots peeled & cut into 1-inch (2.5-cm) pieces

1 _____ large yellow onion, cut into large chunks

1 (14 oz [420 ml]) _____ can of coconut milk

1 cup (240 ml) _____ chicken stock

2 tsp (10 ml) _____ fish sauce, or to taste

2 _____ green onions, sliced

1 _____ large egg

1 tbsp (15 ml) _____ water

1 sheet _____ all-butter puff pastry, defrosted

METHOD

Preheat the oven to 400°F (235°C).

In a large bowl, mix together the chicken, curry powder, sambal, shallot, garlic and lemongrass. Marinate for ½ hour while you prepare the potato, carrots and onions.

Heat up the oil in a large pot over medium-high heat. Add the chicken and brown for 5 minutes. Add the potato, carrots and onion and cook for 5 minutes. Add the coconut milk and chicken stock and bring to a boil, then reduce to a simmer until the vegetables are just cooked, about 20 minutes. Season with fish sauce to taste.

Spoon the curry into an ovenproof dish. In a small bowl, mix together the egg and water. Brush the edges of the dish with the egg wash and press the puff pastry down to cover the curry and seal it in. Brush the top of the puff pastry with the egg wash and cut several small x's for steam vents. Bake until golden and flaky, 15-20 minutes. Let sit for 10 minutes and serve.

BRAISED

· BEEF ·
SHANK

IN RED WINE

BRAISED BEEF SHANK

SERVES: 4

FALL-OFF-THE-BONE RED WINE-BRAISED BEEF

When I was growing up, we didn't eat beef at home. The first thing I did once I moved out and started cooking on my own was go on a beef binge. I'd go to the store and buy random cuts of beef, not knowing what they were or how to cook them. I figured out pretty quickly that slow cooking fatty cuts were delicious, easy and cheap. Braising may take a long time, but the reward is fall-off-the-bone tender beef. I love eating this over mashed potatoes or on its own with some crusty bread for dipping.

INGREDIENTS

1 tbsp (15 ml) _____ oil
1 ½ lbs (680 g) _____ beef shank
as needed _____ salt & freshly ground pepper
1 lb (455 g) _____ mushrooms
1 _____ large onion quartered
8 _____ garlic cloves, peeled, crushed
2 tbsp (30 ml) _____ tomato paste
2 tbsp (30 ml) _____ soy sauce
1 tbsp (15 ml) _____ balsamic vinegar
1 cup (240 ml) _____ red wine
¾ cup (180 ml) _____ cup water
1 _____ sprig rosemary
as needed _____ flat-leaf parsley

METHOD

Preheat the oven to 325°F (160°C).

In a large ovenproof pot or Dutch oven, heat up the oil over medium to medium-high heat. Pat your beef shanks dry, season generously with salt and pepper and when the oil is hot, add to the pot. Sear until a deep brown crust forms, about 5-6 minutes. Repeat on the other side and when done, move to a plate.

If the pot is dry, add a touch of oil and when hot, add the mushrooms, onions and garlic. Stir and cook over medium heat until lightly browned, about 8 minutes. Stir in the tomato paste, soy sauce, and balsamic vinegar. Add the wine, water, browned beef shanks and rosemary. Bring to a boil over high heat and then lower to a simmer. Cover the pot with foil, or oven-proof lid and braise for 4 hours. The shank should be very tender.

Remove the rosemary sprig and discard. Taste and season with salt and pepper if needed. Serve warm with a sprinkle of flat-leaf parsley.

SEAFOOD

Seafood was a staple while I was growing up, back when it was much cheaper than meat. My mom loves seafood and part of the reason I love seafood so much now is because it reminds me of her.

I didn't always love seafood though — when I was young, much to the amusement of my parents, I didn't like fish at all. I had a bad experience with a fish bone once. My parents thought it was hilarious, how I always was the one sitting hungrily at the table while everyone else was ferociously fighting for the best bits of prawns or fish.

I must have grown up, because now I'm fighting right alongside everyone else for the last morsel. I'm not quite sure what was wrong with my younger self, but now I know that bones are nothing to be scared of and that seafood is some of the best food. The best part is its versatility: it can be fast, fresh and easy like the Pan-Roasted Halibut or decadent and elegant like the Miso Glazed Cod.

FISH PIE

SERVES: 4-6

FISH IN BÉCHAMEL, TOPPED WITH MASHED POTATOES

I love potato-topped pies and this fish pie is no exception: the creaminess of the potatoes goes perfectly with the creaminess of the béchamel. Add in carrots, celery and a white fish like tilapia and you have a winner. This is a great dish for a lazy Sunday afternoon, since making béchamel always feels meditative. All that mixing and stirring gives you plenty of time to contemplate life and deliciousness.

INGREDIENTS

1 ½ lbs (675 g) _____ Yukon gold potatoes, peeled and chopped into 1-inch (2.5-cm) pieces

2 tbsp (30 g) _____ butter

¼ cup (60 ml) _____ milk

1 tbsp (15 ml) _____ heavy cream

to taste _____ salt & freshly ground pepper

3 tbsp (45 g) _____ butter

3 tbsp (30 g) _____ all-purpose flour

3 ½ cups (840 ml) _____ milk

2 tbsp (5 g) ___ finely chopped flat-leaf parsley

2 tbsp (5 g) _____ finely chopped dill

1 tbsp (15 ml) _____ oil

1 _____ large onion, diced

2 _____ celery stalks, diced

2 _____ large carrots, diced

2 lbs (900 g) _____ white fish of choice, cut into 1-inch (2.5-cm) pieces

to taste _____ salt & freshly ground pepper

METHOD

Preheat the oven to 400°F (205°C).

To make the mashed potatoes, put the potatoes in a pot and cover them with water. Bring the water to a boil over high heat and lower the heat to simmer the potatoes until fork-tender, about 15-20 minutes.

When your potatoes are tender, drain and mash. Stir in the butter, milk and heavy cream. Taste and season with salt and pepper. Set aside while making the fish pie base.

In a medium saucepot, melt the butter over medium heat. Add the flour and stir constantly over medium heat for about 3 minutes, until smooth. Pour in 1 cup (240 ml) of the milk in a thin stream while whisking. When smooth, add the rest of the milk. Keep on medium heat and stir for about 10 minutes, until the sauce thickens. Add the parsley and chopped dill. Taste and season with salt and pepper. Set aside.

In a large pot, heat the oil over medium-high heat and add the onions, celery and carrot. Cook until tender, 5-7 minutes. Add the fish and cook for 5 minutes, be careful not to break up the pieces too much. Add the béchamel, taste and season with salt and pepper.

Pour the fish mixture into an ovenproof dish and top with the mashed potatoes. Bake for 30 minutes, or until the potatoes are golden and brown. Enjoy warm.

CREAMY DILLY SAUCE

fish pie

BUTTERY MASHED POTATOES

SEAFOOD STEW

SERVES: 2

FISH, SHRIMP, SCALLOPS & CLAMS IN A SPICY TOMATO STEW

Sometimes, in the middle of winter, I'll conflictingly crave something light and clean tasting, but hearty and warming. This bouillabaisse-inspired seafood stew fits the bill perfectly. The spicy, chunky tomato sauce is perfect for scooping up with toasted baguettes and the seafood makes it a lighter alternative to a traditional winter stew. The only problem is that I usually find myself eating twice as much as normal.

INGREDIENTS

2 tbsp (30 ml) _____ oil

1 _____ celery stalk, finely chopped

1 _____ garlic clove, thinly sliced

½ _____ yellow onion, finely chopped

2 tsp (4 g) _____ crushed red pepper

1 cup (240 ml) _____ basic tomato sauce

(page 40)

1 cup (240 ml) _____ white wine

1 _____ large tomato, chopped

1 ___ tilapia filet, cut into 1-inch (2.5-cm) pieces

6 _____ large shrimp

6 _____ large scallops

1 lb (450 g) _____ clams/mussels

4 _____ thick slices of country bread

1 _____ garlic clove

to taste _____ flat-leaf parsley

METHOD

In a large pot, heat the oil over medium heat. Add the celery, garlic, onion and pepper flakes. Cook until translucent, 6 to 8 minutes. Add the tomato sauce, wine and chopped tomato. Bring to a boil. Add the fish and shellfish. Cover and bring to a boil, then uncover and reduce to a simmer until the shellfish have opened, 5-6 minutes. Remove from the heat.

Toast the bread rub with the garlic while still hot. Ladle the seafood stew into bowls and top with a generous sprinkle of parsley. Enjoy immediately.

SEAFOOD STEW

GRILLED

T

FISH TACOS

FISH TACOS

SERVES: 2

PAN-GRILLED FISH WITH LIME & CILANTRO

Fish tacos remind me of oceans, bright white beaches and endless blue skies. In the summer, I love throwing DIY food parties. Everyone gathers at the table to create their own version of the perfect fish taco. Fish tacos are light, filling and super easy to make. Just put out the fish, garnish and a big pile of warmed tacos — everyone can help themselves. This recipe scales up infinitely, so depending on if you're having a party of 2 or 8, adjust accordingly.

INGREDIENTS

1 _____ jalapeño, finely diced

½ _____ onion, finely diced

¼ **cup (10 g)** _____ cilantro, chopped

1 tbsp (15 ml) _____ oil

juice _____ of 1 lime

1 lb (450 g) _____ tilapia or cod, cut into chunks

to taste _____ salt & freshly ground pepper

as needed _____ flour/corn tortillas, warmed

to taste _____ chopped cilantro

to taste _____ finely diced onion

to taste _____ diced tomatoes

to taste _____ hot sauce

to taste _____ lime wedges

METHOD

Combine the jalapeño, onion, cilantro, oil and lime juice. Toss with the tilapia. Heat a bit of oil in a pan over medium high heat and pan-fry fish chunks until cooked, about 3-5 minutes. Season with salt and pepper to taste. Serve fish on warmed tortillas with your choice of the garnishes.

PAN-ROASTED HALIBUT

SERVES: 2-3

SWEET, TENDER HALIBUT WITH LEMON

Fish can be daunting for new cooks, who often overseason and overcook. Simple is best when it comes to fresh fish and especially when it comes to halibut. Mild and slightly sweet with firm flakes, halibut is both decadent and forgiving. It also happens to be my favorite fish to cook because it's so versatile, easy and readily available. I like to pan-roast it in a bit of thyme-infused oil and serve it with lemon wedges.

INGREDIENTS

1 lb (450 g) _____ halibut fillet, cut into 2 or 3 pieces

as needed _____ salt & freshly ground pepper

1 tbsp (15 ml) _____ oil

2 _____ sprigs fresh thyme

to serve _____ lemon wedges

METHOD

Twenty minutes before serving, take the fish out of the fridge to bring it closer to room temperature. Season all sides generously with salt and pepper.

Heat up oil in a frying pan over high heat. When shimmery and hot, add the halibut, turn the heat down to medium-high and cook until golden, about 4-5 minutes. Flip, add the thyme to the pan, cook 4-5 more minutes and serve immediately with lemon wedges.

HALIBUT

IN A POT

CLAM BOIL

with

CLAMS · MUSSELS · SHRIMP
SAUSAGE · CORN

CLAM BOIL

SERVES: 4-6

SAUSAGE, CORN, CLAMS, MUSSELS & SHRIMP IN WHITE WINE

New England clambakes are wondrous things, but when you can't make it to the East Coast, this clam-bake-in-a-pot is the next best thing. There's nothing easier or better than melted butter, fresh corn, sausage, clams, mussels and shrimp in a simple white wine, garlic-thyme stock. Throw down a bunch of newspapers for the shells, gather everyone around the table and get ready to eat a boatload of butter and seafood.

INGREDIENTS

¼ cup (30 g) _____ flaky sea salt

zest _____ of 1 lemon

4 _____ sprigs fresh thyme, leaves only

1 tsp (2 g) _____ crushed red pepper

2 cups (480 ml) _____ white wine

1 ½ lbs (675 g) _____ new potatoes

4 _____ fresh ears of corn, halved

4 _ celery stalks, cut into 1-inch (2.5-cm) pieces

1 lb _____ andouille sausage, cut into 2-inch (5-cm) pieces

1 _____ lemon, quartered

1 _____ head of garlic, peeled & crushed

1 _____ large bunch of thyme

4 lbs (1.8 kg) _____ clams

6 _____ large eggs (optional)

2 lbs (900 g) _____ mussels

2 lbs (900 g) _____ large shrimp

1 cup (230 g) _____ butter, melted

METHOD

In a small bowl, mix together the sea salt, lemon zest, thyme leaves and crushed red pepper. Set aside.

In large pot, bring wine and 6 cups (1.4 l) water to a boil. Add potatoes, cook and cover for 8 minutes. Add the corn, celery, sausage, lemon, garlic, thyme and clams. Cover and cook for 10 minutes, until the clams have opened. Add the eggs if using, mussels and shrimp, and cover. Cook until all the shellfish is open and shrimp are pink, about 6 minutes.

Use a slotted spoon and transfer everything to a large platter. Serve with lemon-thyme salt mix and melted butter.

GRILLED PRAWNS

SERVES: 2

PRAWNS IN FISH SAUCE, LIME & CILANTRO

Living by the Pacific Ocean has its perks: early spring means spot prawn season. We usually end up eating loads and loads every spring. Prawns, spotted or otherwise, are delicious with just a sprinkle of salt, pepper and lemon, but when you have an abundance of prawns, you can afford to get creative. I love the brightness of lime and cilantro in this Vietnamese-style dressing. Sweet and spicy, these prawns are finger-licking good.

INGREDIENTS

1 lb (450 g) _____ large prawns, shell on

juice _____ of 2 limes

2 tsp (10 ml) _____ fish sauce

2 tsp (10 g) _____ sugar

zest _____ of 1 lime

2 _____ Thai chilis, thinly sliced

1 cup (40 g) _____ cilantro, roughly chopped

to taste _____ salt & freshly ground pepper

as needed _____ oil

METHOD

Use a pair of kitchen shears to cut through the backs of the prawn shells and devein them.

In a large bowl, mix together the lime juice, fish sauce and sugar until the sugar is dissolved. Add the zest, chilis and cilantro. Taste and season with salt and freshly ground pepper. Set aside.

Heat up a bit of oil in a frying pan on medium-high heat. When hot, add the prawns and cook them for 2 minutes without moving them in the pan. Flip and continue to cook for 1-2 minutes, until pink and firm. Toss the shrimp in the dressing and let sit for 15 minutes for the flavors to meld. Enjoy warm or chilled.

GRILLED PRAWNS

CRISPY CORNMEAL
FRIED OYSTERS

FRIED OYSTERS

SERVES: 4

CORNMEAL-CRUSTED CRISPY OYSTERS

I love deep-fried oysters and order them whenever I can. Cornmeal is the secret to the crispy yet delicate crusts that give way to creamy, smooth, sea-salty insides. You don't need to fry these guys for too long — just long enough so that the outsides are perfectly golden brown while the insides remain creamy and slightly underdone. These oysters are especially addictive when dipped in a cilantro sriracha aioli.

INGREDIENTS

½ cup (110 g)	mayonnaise
⅓ cup (80 ml)	sriracha
2 tbsp (2.5 g)	chopped cilantro
2 tsp (10 ml)	lime juice
½	garlic clove, minced
as needed	grape seed/rice bran oil
½ cup (65 g)	cornstarch
½ cup (75 g)	cornmeal
¼ tsp	garlic powder
¼ tsp	salt
¼ tsp	freshly ground pepper
1	large egg
1 tbsp (15 ml)	water
2 cups (480 ml)	shucked oysters
to serve	lime wedges

METHOD

To make the aioli, mix together the mayonnaise, sriracha, cilantro, lime juice and garlic in a small bowl. Refrigerate until needed.

Heat 2 inches (5 cm) of oil to 370°F (188°C) over medium heat in a deep pot with tall sides.

While the oil is heating, prepare your oysters. In a bowl, mix together the cornstarch, cornmeal, garlic powder, salt and pepper. In another bowl, mix together the egg and water. Dip the oysters in the cornmeal mix, then the egg, then again in the cornmeal mix.

Add the oysters to the hot oil, 2-3 at a time and fry, flipping once, until golden and crispy, about 1 minute per side. Drain on a wire rack or paper towels and serve immediately with cilantro sriracha aioli and lime wedges.

SHRIMP SALAD ROLLS

SERVES: 3-5

VIETNAMESE RICE PAPER STUFFED WITH SHRIMP CAKES & HERBS

The best times I've had at my in-laws' house are when we gather around the table to make and eat salad rolls. We fill, roll, dip, eat and repeat at leisure, with lots of time in between to chat or share funny anecdotes. These crispy, juicy shrimp cake rolls are a particular favorite. If you're feeling industrious, you can roll these ahead of time, but it's much more fun to have everyone assemble their own rolls at the table, Vietnamese-style.

INGREDIENTS

¼ cup (60 ml) _____ almond butter

¼ cup (60 ml) _____ water

1 tbsp (15 ml) _____ hoisin sauce

juice _____ ½ lime

2 tsp (10 ml) _____ soy sauce

2 tsp (10 ml) _____ sugar

2 tsp (10 ml) _ sambal oelek (chili garlic sauce)

½ tsp _____ toasted sesame oil

1 _____ garlic clove, roughly chopped

1 _____ medium shallot, roughly chopped

¾ lb (340 g) _____ raw baby shrimp, peeled

2 tsp (10 g) _____ sugar

1 tsp (8 g) _____ salt

2 tsp (4 g) _____ freshly ground pepper

2 tbsp (20 g) _____ rice flour

2 tsp (10 ml) _____ oil

15 _____ round rice paper wrappers

15 _____ butter lettuce leaves

4 oz (112 g) _____ cooked rice vermicelli

30 _____ Thai basil leaves

30 _____ mint leaves

15 _____ small sprigs of cilantro

METHOD

To make the dipping sauce, stir together the almond butter, water, hoisin sauce, lime juice, soy sauce, sugar, sambal and sesame oil. Set aside in the fridge.

Blitz the garlic and shallot in a food processor and then add the shrimp, sugar, salt, pepper and rice flour and pulse until it becomes a paste.

Wet your hands and shape the shrimp mixture into 5 patties, about 3 inches (7.5 cm) in diameter.

Heat the oil in a large frying pan over high heat and add the shrimp patties. Fry until golden brown, flipping once, 3 minutes per side. Remove from the pan and slice into 1-inch (2.5-cm) strips.

Take one rice paper wrapper and submerge completely in a large bowl of hot water for 10-15 seconds, until pliable. Place the wrapper on a plate or cutting board. Place a piece of lettuce down, then a bit of vermicelli, 2 Thai basil leaves, 2 mint leaves, a sprig of cilantro and the shrimp cake. Fold the bottom half of the wrapper up over the filling. Hold the fold in place, tuck in the sides and roll. Enjoy with the dipping sauce and repeat.

VIETNAMESE
SHRIMP CAKE
SALAD ROLLS
W/ FRESH HERBS

MISO COD & QUINOA

SERVES: 2

SAIKYO YAKI WITH SESAME SOY QUINOA

Saikyo yaki is a traditional Japanese way of preparing fish and meat by marinating it in white miso from the Kyoto area. It's a popular way of cooking fish for good reason: the sweet and salty miso pairs extremely well with fish, especially black cod. You won't have to go all the way to Kyoto to find miso — most major grocery stores and organic food stores carry it near the tofu. You'll be happy you looked for it when you taste buttery flakes of miso-marinated black cod melting in your mouth.

INGREDIENTS

2 tbsp (30 ml)	sake
2 tbsp (30 ml)	mirin
2 tbsp (14 g)	white miso
1 tbsp (15 g)	sugar
2 (½ lb [225 g])	black cod filets
1 cup (185 g)	cooked quinoa
2 tsp (10 ml)	sesame oil
1 tsp (5 ml)	soy sauce
to taste	toasted sesame seeds
to taste	sliced green onions

METHOD

In a small saucepan, bring the sake and mirin to a boil over medium-high heat. Stir in the miso and sugar, set aside and cool completely.

Pat the cod dry with paper towels and slather on the cooled miso marinade. Place in a deep dish, cover and place in the fridge overnight.

When ready to cook, preheat the oven to 400°F (205°C). Gently wipe off the excess marinade and place the fish in a foil-lined ovenproof dish. Bake for 10-15 minutes, based on thickness. The fish is done when it is opaque and flakes easily. Finish by broiling: turn the broiler on high and watch carefully as the top caramelizes and turns a deep golden brown. Remove and enjoy immediately with the sesame soy quinoa.

To make the sesame soy quinoa, gently toss together the quinoa, sesame oil and soy sauce. Taste and adjust sesame oil and soy if needed. Top with sesame seeds and green onions.

VEGETABLES

Vegetables are where flavors are formed in cooking. It's hard not to love the texture, flavors and colors vegetables bring to the table. My go-to for vegetables, aside from having them in their beautiful raw state, is roasting. Roasting vegetables intensifies their flavors, caramelizes their outsides and generally brings out their natural sweetness. Oven-Roasted Sprouts with pine nuts and parmesan will convert any brussels sprout hater and roasted Dijon Mushrooms with lemon and will convince you that you don't miss meat.

ROSEMARY POTATOES

SERVES: 4-6

ROASTED POTATOES WITH CRISPY, CRUNCHY EDGES & FLUFFY INSIDES

I am a straight-up unabashed potato lover. Baked, boiled, fried, mashed, scalloped, shredded or steamed: I love them all. I think I could eat an entire meal of potatoes. For me, the best potatoes are when multiple textures are combined. These oven-roasted potatoes are a good representation of how fantastic potatoes can be. Their crunchy crusts give way to creamy, fluffy insides.

INGREDIENTS

4-6 _____ large russet potatoes, peeled and cut into 2-inch (5-cm) chunks

1 tsp (8 g) _____ salt

⅓ cup (80 ml) _____ grape seed/rice bran oil

2 _____ sprigs fresh rosemary, needles only, chopped

to taste _____ salt & freshly ground pepper

METHOD

Preheat the oven to 475°F (245°C).

Place the potatoes in a large pot and cover with water. Add the salt and bring to a boil over high heat. Reduce to a simmer and cook until just fork tender, 15 minutes. Drain and place the potatoes back in the pot, shaking to rough up them up for extra crispy edges.

Pour the oil into a deep metal roasting tin and place in the oven for 10 minutes. The oil will be very hot, so be careful as you take the pan out of the oven and add the potatoes to the hot oil.

Turn the temperature down to 400°F (205°C). Sprinkle on the chopped rosemary and return to the oven. Roast for 50 minutes to 1 hour, or until crispy and deeply golden brown, turning halfway through. Enjoy hot with a sprinkling of salt and pepper.

Note: If you happen to have duck fat around, use it in lieu of the oil and you'll be blown away by the flavor and crunch.

CRISPY ROAST · ROSEMARY

Potatoes

CRUNCHY & FLUFFY

DIJON MUSHROOMS

SERVES: 2

OVEN-ROASTED MUSHROOMS WITH GARLIC, LEMON & DIJON

Turning up the oven and baking something is a surefire way to make your house feel a little homier. Roasting mushrooms is awesome for the same reason. The oven heats up your kitchen, making it warm and cozy, and the earthy, delicious smell definitely gets your appetite going. These roasted mushrooms, lusciously coated with butter, garlic and dijon mustard are a perfect little afternoon snack or side dish, especially with lots of hot, toasty bread.

INGREDIENTS

1 lb (450 g) _____ mushrooms

3 _____ garlic cloves, minced

1 _____ small shallot, minced

2 tbsp (30 ml) _____ oil

2 tbsp (30 g) _____ butter

2 tsp (10 ml) _____ lemon juice

¼ cup (15 g) _____ chopped flat-leaf parsley

1 tbsp (15 ml) _____ dijon mustard

to taste _____ salt & freshly ground pepper

if desired _____ toasted bread

METHOD

Preheat the oven to 450°F (235°C).

Clean, trim and halve or quarter the mushrooms. Toss the mushrooms, garlic and shallots in the oil and place in an ovenproof dish. Top with the butter and roast, stirring occasionally, until the mushrooms are tender and deeply browned, about 20-25 minutes. Stir in the lemon juice, parsley and dijon. Taste and season with salt and pepper. Enjoy immediately with crusty bread, if desired.

DIJON MUSHROOMS

LIGHT AND CRISPY

CORN TEMPURA

W/ SHICHIMI TOGARASHI

CORN FRITTERS

SERVES: 2

TEMPURA CORN FRITTERS WITH A SPRINKLE OF JAPANESE SEVEN-SPICE

Corn tempura is the freshest, most satisfying corn fritter you'll ever taste. The sweet juiciness of the corn is accented by the crispness of the tempura batter. For crispy tempura, the key is to have all of your ingredients prepped and your oil hot before mixing the batter. If you make your batter too early, it gives it a chance to develop gluten, which is tempura's mortal enemy. For the same reason, make sure you use icy cold water when mixing with the egg whites.

INGREDIENTS

as needed _____ grape seed/rice bran oil

⅓ cup (50 g) _____ all-purpose flour

½ tsp _____ baking soda

1 _____ large egg white

⅓ cup (80 ml) _____ icy cold water

2 ears _____ fresh corn, cut off the cob

¼ _____ sheet roasted nori, cut into strips

to taste _____ shichimi togarashi
(Japanese seven-spice mix)

METHOD

Set up a wire rack inside a rimmed tray or line a plate with paper towels.

Preheat 1 ½ inches (3.8 cm) of oil to 375°F (190°C) over medium heat in a pot with tall sides.

In a small bowl, mix the flour and baking soda together. In another bowl, whisk together the egg whites and water. Add the wet mix to the dry and stir until just mixed. Stir in the corn, and nori strips.

Gently drop the corn batter into the oil by the spoonful. Deep fry, turning once, until golden brown, 2-3 minutes. Drain on your rack or plate, sprinkle with shichimi togarashi and enjoy immediately.

Note: You can find shichimi togarashi at most grocery stores in the International aisle. It's also called nana-iro togarashi.

CELERY
CUCUMBER
SALAD

CUCUMBER CELERY SALAD

SERVES: 2-4

CRUNCHY CUCUMBERS & CELERY IN A SPICY DRESSING

I once spent an extra hot summer travelling through Asia with my parents. The heat was so oppressive that I didn't even think about eating. The only thing that could tempt me was garlic cucumber salad. Cool and crunchy, I subsisted on them for days. This cucumber dish is perfect when you're looking for something refreshing to pique your appetite. Cucumber salads are quick, satisfying, and provide a cooling counterpoint to spicier dishes.

INGREDIENTS

2 tbsp (30 ml) _____ rice vinegar

1 tbsp (15 ml) _____ sesame oil

2 tsp (10 g) _____ sugar

2 _____ small cucumbers
or ½ large cucumber, sliced

3 _____ celery stalks, thinly sliced

½ cup (20 g) _____ chopped cilantro

1 _____ green onion, sliced

2 _____ garlic cloves, crushed, then minced

1 _____ Thai chili, thinly sliced (optional)

to taste _____ salt

to taste _____ crushed red pepper

to taste _____ toasted sesame seeds

METHOD

In a large bowl, whisk together the rice vinegar, sesame oil and sugar. Add the cucumber, celery, cilantro, green onion and garlic. Add the Thai chili (if using). Toss until evenly dressed, taste and season with salt and red pepper flakes. Sprinkle with sesame seeds and enjoy immediately, or chill to enjoy later.

ROASTED VEGETABLES

SERVES: 4

SLOW-ROASTED VEGETABLES WITH ROSEMARY & THYME

Oven roasting is an essential technique for any cook. Roasting vegetables is a great hands-off way to make a delicious side or main that essentially is vegetable candy. You can pretty much roast any vegetable and it will come out fantastic. The trick is to make sure it's cut in uniform pieces and coated evenly with oil, which ensures even cooking and caramelization. Eating your vegetables has never been so sweet.

INGREDIENTS

6 _____ garlic cloves, peeled & crushed
2 _____ carrots
1 _____ onion
2 _____ red peppers
1 _____ small zucchini
1 _____ small eggplant
1 _____ bunch of asparagus
3 tbsp (45 ml) _____ oil
1 _____ sprig fresh rosemary
3 _____ sprigs fresh thyme
to taste _____ salt & freshly ground pepper

METHOD

Preheat the oven to 425°F (220°C).

Cut the vegetables into 1-inch (2.5-cm) pieces.

Toss the vegetables in the oil and place in an ovenproof dish. Top with the rosemary and thyme. Bake until the vegetables are brown and tender, stirring every 10 minutes, 25-35 minutes total. Season with salt and pepper to taste and enjoy immediately.

OVEN ▽ ROASTED

VEGETABLES

ROSEMARY & THYME

OVEN
ROASTED
BRUSSELS SPROUTS
W/ PINE NUTS AND PARMESAN

OVEN-ROASTED SPROUTS

SERVES: 4

CARAMELIZED SPROUTS WITH PARMESAN, PINE NUTS & LEMON

One year, for Christmas dinner, I told my mom I'd bring brussels sprouts. In a strange role reversal of mother and daughter, she told me no one would want to eat them. She was pretty much convinced that my sprouts would languish in the corner, to be forgotten and forced upon an unlucky cousin to take home in a tin foil pouch. In reality, my crispy, caramelized oven-roasted sprouts dish was one of the first to disappear.

INGREDIENTS

1 lb (450 g) _____ brussels sprouts

2 tbsp (30 ml) _____ oil

2 tsp (10 ml) _____ fresh lemon juice

2 tbsp (11.25 g) _____ freshly grated parmesan

2 tbsp (16 g) _____ toasted pine nuts

to taste _____ salt & freshly ground pepper

METHOD

Preheat the oven to 400°F (205°C).

Trim the ends off the sprouts, wash and cut in half. Toss the brussels sprouts with the oil and roast, cut-side down, on a rimmed metal baking sheet for 35-40 minutes, until deeply browned. When tender and crispy, remove from the oven. Toss with the lemon juice, parmesan and pine nuts. Taste and season with salt and pepper. Enjoy immediately.

GRILLED CORN

SERVES: 4

CHAR-GRILLED CORN BRUSHED WITH SOY SAUCE & BUTTER

Corn on the cob is one of summer's simple pleasures. Sitting by the barbecue with corn juice dripping down your chin and the late sun fading into the horizon just can't be beat. Add some soy sauce and butter and your head just might explode from the deliciousness. The natural sweetness of corn is highlighted with butter, soy and a bit of spice. This just may be your new favorite way to eat corn.

INGREDIENTS

2 tbsp (30 ml) _____ soy sauce

2 tbsp (30 ml) _____ mirin

¼ cup (60 ml) _____ butter, melted

4 ears _____ corn, husks on

to taste _____ shichimi togarashi (Japanese seven-spice mix)

METHOD

Preheat the grill to medium.

Stir the soy sauce, mirin and melted butter together in a small bowl. Set aside.

Prepare the corn by pulling the husks down to the base of the ear without removing. Strip away all the corn silk and fold the husks back into place. Soak the corn in water for 10 minutes.

Remove the ears from the water and shake off the excess water. Place the corn on the grill, cover and cook for 15-20 minutes, turning every 5 minutes. Carefully remove the husks and brush with the soy sauce mixture. Sprinkle with shichimi togarashi and enjoy immediately.

MISO EGGPLANT

SERVES: 2-4

OVEN-ROASTED EGGPLANT WITH CARAMELIZED MISO

When you bake eggplant, it softens and sweetens into a delicious melty mess with a wonderful texture. Add in a bit of caramelization and you've got a dish reminiscent of crème brûlée, only with a sweet and salty miso crust and a creamy eggplant custard. With its sugar crust, this dish never fails to impress.

INGREDIENTS

1 tbsp (15 ml) _____ mirin

1 tbsp (15 ml) _____ sake

2 tbsp (14 g) _____ shiro miso

2 tbsp (30 g) _____ sugar

2 ___ Japanese eggplants, cut in half lengthwise

½ tsp _____ sesame oil

to taste _____ toasted sesame seeds

to taste _____ sliced green onions

METHOD

Place the mirin and sake in a small saucepan and bring to a simmer over medium heat for 2 minutes. Add the miso and stir until smooth. Stir in the sugar, and reduce to very low heat. Continue to cook, stirring occasionally, while you broil the eggplants.

Brush the cut sides of the eggplants with the sesame oil. Put the eggplants cut-side down on a baking sheet and place in the oven and roast for 15-20 minutes (depending on eggplant size) until just starting to shrivel. The flesh should be fork tender. Remove from the oven and turn them over.

Top the eggplants with the miso sauce and put them under the broiler until the sauce bubbles up and starts to caramelize, 1-2 minutes. Remove from heat, rest for 5 minutes and enjoy with sesame seeds and green onions.

SOUPS & STEWS

I made my first pot of soup when I was fifteen. It was a huge failure. My parents went on vacation, leaving my older brother and me at home to fend for ourselves. I thought I'd try to make a chicken and wild rice soup. I didn't bother looking up a recipe and just threw a bunch of things in a pot with water. I set the heat on high and went to watch TV, thinking that my soup would be ready by the time I was done. One episode turned into another and soon my brother ran into the living room to ask me what was burning. We rushed to the kitchen where we found my pot of soup: a charred, blackened, dry mess that had fused to the pot. We threw the pot away and that was the end of my soup career — for a while at least.

Soup is actually quite easy to master, as long as you have the patience and don't set the heat too high. I love soups in all their consistencies: thick and chunky Salmon Dill Chowder, or smooth and creamy Carrot Coconut Curry. I especially love noodles in soup: Miso Chicken Ramen and Ginger Chicken Noodle are always fast favorites.

SHIRO MISO

CHICKEN
•RAMEN•

CORN, SPINACH, EGG

MISO CHICKEN RAMEN

SERVES: 2

CHICKEN & NOODLES IN A SAVORY MISO BROTH

My standard snack in high school was half a pack of chicken instant ramen. I loved the neon yellow glow of the "chicken" broth. I rarely indulge in instant ramen anymore; instead I spend a few extra minutes whipping up a quick bowl of homemade miso chicken ramen. This recipe is super simple and the best part is that you can basically top it with almost anything you have in the fridge. I like to keep it classic with a soft-boiled egg, buttered corn, spinach, poached chicken and green onions.

INGREDIENTS

2 _____ large eggs, room temp

1 _____ large bowl filled with cold water & ice

6 cups (1.44 l) ___ low-sodium chicken stock or Asian Chicken Noodle Stock (page 149)

2 tbsp (14 g) _____ shiro miso, or to taste

1 tbsp (15 g) _____ butter

1 cup (250 g) _____ corn

2 cups (170 g) _____ raw spinach

2 servings _____ fresh/dry ramen noodles

1 ½ cups (225 g) ___ shredded poached chicken (page 196)

1 _____ onion, thinly sliced

to taste _____ sliced green onions

to taste _____ seaweed

to taste _____ sesame oil

METHOD

To soft boil the eggs, bring a pot of water with 3 inches (7.6 cm) of water up to a boil over high heat. Reduce the heat until the water is barely simmering. Using a slotted spoon, gently add your eggs and set a timer for 6 minutes. When the 6 minutes are up, use the slotted spoon to remove the eggs and immediately plunge into the ice water bath. Let cool completely. When cool, gently crack and peel under cold running water and set aside.

Heat up the chicken stock in a stockpot over medium heat. Stir in the miso paste (miso varies in saltiness, so taste and adjust accordingly).

In a small frying pan, heat the butter over medium heat and add the corn. Stir to coat each kernel of corn in butter. Set aside.

Briefly blanch the spinach in boiling water. Cook the ramen noodles according to the package. Drain and divide noodles into 2 deep bowls. Top each bowl with shredded chicken, the prepared spinach and corn, thinly sliced onions, and one of the soft-boiled eggs sliced in half. Ladle on the soup. Serve with green onions, seaweed and sesame oil, to taste.

Note: Shiro miso is white miso, which is milder and smoother than regular miso. You can usually find it in the refrigerated section near the tofu or at organic/health food stores.

MUSHROOM BARLEY

SERVES: 6

ROASTED MUSHROOMS & PEARLED BARLEY SOUP

I'm a sucker for making my home as warm and cozy as possible in the winter, which I usually achieve by turning up the oven all day long. This soup is a great example of my perfect lazy winter's day meal. Roasting the mushrooms gives this soup an extra earthiness that you don't get if you just sauté. It may be an extra step, but it's well worth the flavor, not to the mention the delicious mushroom smell that permeates your whole house while you curl up with a good cookbook.

INGREDIENTS

1 lb (450 g) _____ cremini mushrooms, sliced

½ lb (225 g) _____ shitake mushrooms, sliced

2 tbsp (30 ml) _____ oil

1 tbsp (15 ml) _____ oil

1 _____ medium onion, diced

3 _____ celery stalks, diced

1 _____ garlic clove, minced

6 cups (960 ml) _____ low-sodium beef stock

2 cups (480 ml) _____ water

1 cup (210 g) _____ pearled barley

2 _____ sprigs fresh thyme

to taste _____ salt & freshly ground pepper

3 tbsp (11 g) _____ chopped flat-leaf parsley

METHOD

Preheat the oven to 425°F (220°C).

Toss mushrooms in oil and roast in a single layer on a foil-lined baking sheet until deeply golden brown, 25-30 minutes.

In a large stockpot, heat the oil over medium heat. When hot and shimmery, add the onion and celery. Cook, stirring occasionally, for 5-8 minutes, until the onions and celery are soft but not browned. Add the garlic and cook for 1 minute. Add the roasted mushrooms plus the beef stock, water, barley and fresh thyme. Bring to a boil and then lower to a rolling simmer, covering the soup partially with a lid for 35-40 minutes. The barley should be soft and fully cooked when done. If the soup is too thick for your liking, add more stock. Taste, add the flat-leaf parsley, season with salt and pepper and enjoy warm.

MUSHROOM BARLEY

CURRY

CARROT
COCONUT

SOUP

CARROT COCONUT CURRY

SERVES: 3-4

SMOOTH & CREAMY CARROT SOUP

I don't buy a lot of kitchen gadgets because they tend to sit unused and forgotten in a cupboard. I never thought I'd fall in love with an immersion blender, but when I received one as a gift I realized how awesome they are. I love the creaminess of smooth soups and immersion blenders make it super-easy to smooth out a soup right in the pot. This slightly spicy coconut and carrot soup is smooth, creamy, gluten-free and vegan, but best of all, it's incredibly delicious.

INGREDIENTS

1 tbsp (15 ml) _____ oil
½ _____ onion, diced
1 tbsp (6 g) _____ minced ginger
4 cups (520 g) _____ chopped carrots, about 4-5 carrots
2 ½ cups (600 ml) ____ vegetable stock, divided
1 (14 oz [414 ml]) _____ can coconut milk
2 tbsp (30 ml) _____ red curry paste
to taste _____ salt and freshly ground pepper

as needed _____ chopped cilantro
as needed _____ lime wedges
as needed _____ crushed red pepper

METHOD

In a medium stockpot, heat up the oil over medium heat. Add the onions and sauté until translucent, about 6-7 minutes. Add the ginger, carrots and 1 ½ cups (360 ml) of vegetable stock. Bring to a boil, then lower to a simmer. Cover and cook with a lid until carrots are tender, about 15-20 minutes.

When the carrots are soft, carefully blend in a blender or with an immersion blender until the carrots are smooth. Return carrot mixture to the pot and add the rest of the vegetable stock along with the coconut milk and red curry paste. Stir until well blended. Simmer gently for 10 minutes. Season with salt and pepper to taste.

Serve with cilantro, lime wedges and red pepper flakes, if desired.

ROASTED JALAPEÑO CHILI

SERVES: 4-6

BEEF & PORK WITH CHARRED JALAPEÑOS & TOASTED CORIANDER

Thursdays were my favorite day at school. It was one day away from Friday, but even better, Thursdays meant chili for lunch. My eight-year-old self thought it was the best thing ever. Real Texas chili made with steak is delicious too, but lunchroom chili made with ground meat will always hold a special place in my heart. I spiced this one up with charred jalapeños and toasted coriander seeds to add a bit more flavor to an old favorite.

INGREDIENTS

3 _____ jalapeños
1 tbsp (6 g) _____ coriander seeds
1 tbsp (15 ml) _____ oil
1 lb (450 g) _____ ground pork
1 lb (450 g) _____ ground beef
1 _____ onion, chopped
2 _____ garlic cloves, chopped
1 _____ large red pepper, chopped
2 _____ carrots, diced
2 _____ celery stalks, diced
2 tsp (6 g) _____ cumin
2 tsp (8 g) _____ cayenne
1 tsp (2 g) _____ paprika
1 tbsp (6 g) ___ crushed red pepper, or to taste
1 ½ cups (360 ml) _____ beef stock
¼ cup (60 ml) _____ tomato paste
2 (14.5 oz [428 ml]) _____ cans diced tomatoes
to taste _____ salt & freshly ground pepper

to taste _____ sliced green onions
to taste _____ sour cream
to taste _____ shredded cheddar

METHOD

Place the jalapeños on a foil lined baking sheet. Place under the broiler until the skins are charred, about 7-10 minutes. Place in a bowl and cover with saran wrap for 10 minutes. When cool, slip off the skins, halve and slice. If adverse to spice, remove the seeds. Set aside.

Toast the coriander seeds in a dry nonstick skillet over medium heat until fragrant. Crush seeds with a mortar and pestle and set aside.

Heat oil in a large stockpot over medium-high heat. Add the pork and beef and cook until deeply browned, about 10 minutes. Break up the meat using a wooden spoon. Remove meat from the pot and drain off all the fat leaving about 1 tablespoon (15 ml) behind. Add the onion to the oil and sauté until brown, about 6 minutes. Add the garlic, red pepper, carrots, celery and spices to the pot. Sauté, stirring occasionally until the vegetables are cooked, about 8 minutes. Add the meat back in as well as the beef stock, tomato paste, diced tomatoes and jalapeños. Bring to a boil and then lower heat and simmer for 1 hour until chili thickens. Taste and season with salt and pepper if needed. Serve warm with green onions, sour cream and cheddar.

ROASTED JALAPEÑO
CHILI CON CARNE

CRAB & CAULIFLOWER

SERVES: 4

CAULIFLOWER, POTATO & CRAB SOUP

My most delicious recipes often come from my favorite source: Mike. Mostly he comes up with crazy concoctions that I'd never even consider trying, but sometimes his ideas are spot on. This creamy cauliflower soup is an old favorite of mine, but Mike always refused to eat it because it doesn't have any "meat" in it. One day he suggested adding crab. The contrast between the crab chunks and smoothness of the cauliflower and potato makes this version even better than the original.

INGREDIENTS

1 lb (450 g) _____ snow crab legs

1 _____ large bowl cold water & ice

1 tbsp (15 ml) _____ oil

1 _____ medium onion, quartered

2 _____ garlic cloves, sliced

6 cups (1.4 l) _____ water

1 _____ small head of cauliflower cut into florets, about 6 cups (600 g) florets

1 _____ large baking potato, cut into chunks

to taste _____ salt & freshly ground pepper

to serve _____ chopped cilantro

METHOD

Bring water in a steamer pot to boil over high heat. Place the crab legs in the steamer and steam for 7 minutes. The shells will be orange when they're done. Remove and plunge into an ice bath. De-shell the crab, reserving the shells. Set aside the crab meat in the fridge.

In a large stockpot, heat the oil over medium heat. Add the crab shells, onion and garlic and sauté, about 3-4 minutes. Add the water, bring to a boil, then reduce heat and simmer for 45 minutes to an hour, skimming off foam.

After the stock is done, strain out the solids and return to the pot. Add the cauliflower and potato. Simmer until very tender, about 30-35 minutes. Purée until smooth using an immersion blender. Stir in half of the reserved crab, taste and season with salt and pepper. If too thick, thin out with water, ¼ cup (60 ml) at a time. Serve immediately with chopped cilantro.

CAULIFLOWER

SMOOTH · CREAMY

CRAB SOUP

SALMON DILL CHOWDER

SERVES: 4-6

SPICY CHOWDER WITH DIJON & DILL

I wish I could tell a story about how my dad used to take me fishing for salmon and my mom would make this fabulous salmon chowder out of our catch, but in reality I've never even been fishing. Instead, what I can say about this soup is that it's delicious. Dill goes fantastically well with fish and this chowder is loaded with it. This is the kind of soup that reminds you of summer, even if you're eating it in the middle of a winter storm.

INGREDIENTS

1 tbsp (15 ml) _____ oil
1 _____ carrot, diced
2 _____ celery stalks, diced
6 cups (1.4 l) _____ chicken stock
2 ½ cups (250 g) _____ cauliflower florets
12 oz (340 g) _____ salmon fillet,
              cut into ½-inch (1.3-cm) chunks
2 tbsp (10.5 g) _____ sliced green onions
¼ cup (2.25 g) _____ fresh dill, roughly chopped
1 tbsp (15 ml) _____ dijon mustard
1 _____ jalapeño, diced
1 cup (50 g) _____ instant mashed potato flakes
to taste _____ salt & freshly ground pepper

METHOD

In a medium stockpot, heat up the oil on medium to medium-high heat. Add the carrot and celery and cook, about 7-8 minutes. Add the stock and cauliflower and bring to a boil. Lower to a simmer for 10 minutes then add the salmon, green onions, dill, dijon and jalapeño. Simmer for 5 minutes. Stir in the potato flakes, season with salt and pepper and serve warm.

Note: when buying instant mashed potatoes, take a look at the ingredients and buy a package that lists only potatoes. Instant mashed potato flakes add creaminess and thickness to this soup. Feel free to use leftover mashed potatoes if you don't have any potato flakes on hand.

SALMON DILL CHOWDER

GINGER CHICKEN NOODLE

SERVES: 4

THIN RICE NOODLES IN A SAVORY GINGER CHICKEN BROTH

I grew up eating a different kind of chicken noodle soup than the average kid. The homemade version that my mom made was more of a simple, clear chicken broth with a slightly spicy ginger flavor, full of rice noodles, mushrooms and greens. As an adult, this dish never fails to remind me of home and growing up. It's also perfect for those days when you're feeling just a bit under the weather — the ginger is sure to make you feel better.

INGREDIENTS

1.5 lbs (680 g) _____ chicken bones

8 cups (1.9 l) _____ water

3-4" (8-10 cm) _____ fresh ginger, peeled & sliced

1 bunch _____ green onions

1 bunch _____ cilantro

to taste _____ salt

4 cups (340 g) _____ raw spinach/leafy green

8 _____ shiitake mushrooms, thinly sliced

4 servings _____ rice noodles of your choice

4 cups (600 g) ____ shredded poached chicken (page 196)

4 _____ soft-boiled eggs (page 137)

¼ cup (21 g) _____ sliced green onions

METHOD

Put chicken bones in a medium stockpot and barely cover with water. Bring to a boil and keep at high heat for 5 minutes to boil out the impurities. Rinse off the bones and give the pot a good wash. Fill the pot with 8 cups (2 l) of cold water, then add the rinsed-off bones and the ginger, green onions and cilantro. Bring to a boil and then reduce to a simmer for 2 hours.

Strain out the solids and season the broth with salt to taste. Return soup to the pot and keep on a gentle simmer while assembling your noodle bowl.

Briefly blanch the spinach and shiitakes in boiling water. Cook the rice noodles according to the package. Drain, and divide noodles into four deep bowls. Top equally with shredded chicken, the prepared spinach, shiitake mushrooms and a soft-boiled egg sliced in half. Ladle on the soup. Serve with green onions and your favorite hot sauce and soy sauce, if preferred.

BEEF

— & —

GUINNESS

a hearty stew

BEEF & GUINNESS

SERVES: 4

TENDER BEEF SHORT RIBS & MUSHROOMS IN STOUT & STOCK

I love the classic, well-executed British fare you get at London pubs: cottage pies, sausage and mash and, of course, Guinness stew. If you're not a fan of beer, don't worry: eating this stew is nothing like drinking a pint. The stout cooks down and gives the short ribs a deep, complex flavor that makes you want more and more. If you have the time, make this stew the day before you're planning on eating it. It tastes even better the day after.

INGREDIENTS

1 ½ lbs (675 g) _____ boneless beef short ribs, cut into 1-inch (2.5-cm) pieces

1 tbsp (10 g) _____ all-purpose flour

½ tsp _____ salt

¼ tsp _____ freshly ground pepper

1 tbsp (15 ml) _____ oil

½ _____ large onion, coarsely chopped

1 _____ large carrot, large dice

2 _ celery stalks, cut into 1-inch (2.5-cm) pieces

1 lb (450 g) ____ cremini mushrooms, quartered

1 _____ garlic clove, minced

1 tbsp (15 ml) _____ tomato paste

2 cups (480 ml) _____ beef stock

1 (12 oz [355 ml]) _____ bottle of Guinness

2 tsp (10 ml) _____ Worcestershire sauce

1 tsp (4 g) _____ capers

2 _____ sprigs fresh thyme

to taste _____ salt & freshly ground pepper

METHOD

Preheat the oven to 350°F (180°C).

Pat the beef dry with a paper towel. In a medium bowl, stir together the flour, salt and pepper. Add the beef to the flour and toss to coat. Shake excess flour off the beef and set aside. Heat oil in an ovenproof pot over medium heat until oil is hot and shimmery. Brown the meat deeply without overcrowding, turning occasionally, about 5 minutes per batch. Transfer to a bowl.

Over medium heat, add the onion, carrot, celery, mushrooms and garlic to the pot and cook, scraping up brown bits. Stir frequently until slightly cooked, about 6-8 minutes. Add the cooked beef with juices, along with the tomato paste, stock, beer, Worcestershire sauce, capers and thyme. Bring to a simmer, then cover and transfer to oven. Braise until beef is very tender and sauce has thickened, about 1 ½-2 hours. Season with salt and pepper to taste. Serve warm on its own or with mashed potatoes or crusty bread.

TOMATO EGG DROP

SERVES: 3-4

SILKY EGG DROP SOUP WITH TOMATOES & PORK

One year, Mike and I had the bright idea to visit New York City in the dead of winter. We arrived in the middle of a major snowstorm, but that didn't stop us from braving the weather to find something delicious to eat. We found a tiny soup shop a couple of blocks from the hotel and their egg drop soup was just what we needed. Egg drop soup was the first thing I made when we got back home. It whips up in under half an hour, so it's perfect when you're looking for something heartwarming and fast.

INGREDIENTS

1 tbsp (15 ml) _____ oil

¼ lb (112 g) _____ ground pork

2 _____ garlic cloves, finely diced

1 lb (450 g) _____ ripe tomatoes, chopped

5 cups (1.2 l) _____ water

2 tsp (10 g) _____ sugar

2 tbsp (10.5 g) _____ sliced green onions

to taste _____ salt & white pepper

2 _____ large eggs, lightly beaten

to serve _____ sliced green onions

METHOD

In a medium stockpot, heat the oil over medium heat. When shimmering, add the pork and garlic. Break up the pork and lightly brown, about 7-8 minutes. Add the tomatoes and cook on high for 5 minutes. Add the water, sugar and green onions. Bring to a simmer for 15 minutes. Turn off the heat and drizzle in the eggs in a thin stream while stirring. Taste and season with salt and white pepper to taste. Serve with green onions on top.

CHICKEN
TORTILLA
SOUP

CHICKEN TORTILLA

SERVES: 4-6

CHICKEN, AVOCADO & CRISPY TORTILLAS IN A SPICY TOMATO BROTH

I have a weakness for the tortilla chips you get at Mexican restaurants. It took me the longest time to figure out why their tortilla chips taste so much better than the ones you buy at the store. When I learned that they were old tortillas, deep fried, I went a bit crazy frying up batch after batch of fresh chips. This soup is delicious in its own right, with tender chunks of chicken and spicy tomato broth, but for me, it's just a vehicle for hot, crispy, deliciously fresh chips.

INGREDIENTS

1 tbsp (30 ml) _____ oil

1 _____ onion, diced

3 _____ garlic cloves, minced

1 tbsp (7.5 g) _____ powdered pasilla chili
(or ancho chili powder)

1 _____ medium Anaheim chili, chopped

1 (14.5 oz [428 ml]) can _____ fire-roasted
diced tomatoes

8 cups (1.9 l) _____ low-sodium chicken stock

to taste _____ salt & freshly ground pepper

6 _____ boneless, skinless chicken thighs,
poached and shredded (page 196)

as desired _____ fresh tortillas

as needed _____ grape-seed/rice bran oil

to garnish _____ sliced jalapeños

to garnish _____ cilantro, roughly chopped

to garnish _____ avocado, sliced

to garnish _____ shredded cheddar

to garnish _____ sour cream

to garnish _____ crunchy tortilla strips

to garnish _____ lime wedges

METHOD

In a medium stockpot, heat the oil over medium heat. Add the onion and cook until translucent but not brown, about 5 minutes. Add the garlic, chili powder and Anaheim chili. Cook for 1 minute. Add the tomatoes and chicken stock. Bring to a boil over high heat and then reduce to a low simmer for 15 minutes. Add the shredded chicken and heat until warmed. Season with salt and pepper to taste.

While the soup is simmering, heat up 1-inch (2.5-cm) of oil to 350°F (175°C) in a deep pot over medium heat. Line a large plate with paper towels. Cut the tortillas into thin strips. When the oil is hot, add a handful of strips and fry until golden brown, 1-2 minutes. Remove with tongs or a slotted spoon and drain on the lined plate.

To serve, add tortilla strips to each bowl of soup. Top with garnishes to taste.

ROASTED CORN & TOMATO

SERVES: 3-4

ROASTED TOMATO, CORN & BACON CHOWDER

When I was ten, I visited a cornfield for the first time. Unfortunately we arrived at dusk, when the shadows were ominous and the rows of corn looked more menacing than delicious. I didn't pick any corn that trip, opting to stay in the safety of the pickup truck instead. Later, safe at home, my mom made a quick corn chowder so delicous it made me wish that I had contributed to our little harvest. Freshly picked corn is so delicious that cooking it almost seems a travesty, but this chowder is worth it.

INGREDIENTS

2 ears _____ fresh corn, husked

2 _____ medium tomatoes

4 _ slices bacon, chopped in 1-inch (2.5-cm) pieces

1 _____ onion, diced

2 _____ celery stalks, diced

2 _____ potatoes, peeled & diced

1 _____ serrano pepper, finely chopped

3 cups (720 ml) _____ chicken stock

to taste _____ salt & freshly ground pepper

METHOD

In a large dry nonstick pan, roast the corn and tomatoes on medium-high heat until charred and blistered, about 10-15 minutes. Be sure to rotate the corn and tomatoes so they brown evenly.

When cool to touch, cut the corn off the cob and roughly chop the tomatoes. Set aside.

In a medium stockpot, cook the bacon over medium heat. When crispy, remove the excess fat and add the onion, celery and potatoes, making sure to scrape up the brown bits from the bottom of the pan.

Add tomatoes and corn, along with the serrano and stock. Bring to a boil and then lower the heat and simmer for 15-20 minutes. Season with salt and pepper to taste and serve warm.

Note: If you have a bundt pan, use it to catch your corn kernels. Wedge the pointy end of the corn into the hole of the bundt pan, hold the top of the cob firmly and slice top to bottom. The corn will fall neatly into the pan.

ROASTED

CORN & TOMATO SOUP

SANDWICHES

When I was a kid, I disliked all sandwiches aside from my beloved peanut butter and jelly. I didn't realize until I was in my teens that sandwiches could be more than two pieces of white bread with a smear of mayonnaise and a single slice of grocery store bologna. It was a true epiphany when I had a perfectly made sandwich where each bite was a balanced combination of textures and flavors. Now I love sandwiches. There's something so magical about they way you get a bit of everything in each bite — and bonus, no utensils required! Nothing says "I love you" like a well-made sandwich, so go ahead and love yourself with a crispy, gooey French Onion Grilled Cheese, hearty and savory Lamb and Peas or decadent Porchetta and Salsa Verde on ciabatta.

PORCHETTA

SANDWICH

PORCHETTA & SALSA VERDE

MAKES: 2

JUICY TENDER ROASTED PORK WITH CRISPY CRACKLING & SALSA VERDE

There's a sandwich shop near my house that's famous for its porchetta. The sandwiches are addictive: juicy pork, crispy crackling and pesto all on top of a freshly baked ciabatta bun. They're messy, delicious and satisfying. After tasting one, I knew I needed to recreate it at home. These sandwiches are the ultimate reward for making your own porchetta (page 73) and they may be the best sandwiches to ever come out of your kitchen — they're just that good.

INGREDIENTS

2 tsp (4 g) _____ fennel seeds

2 tsp (4 g) _____ coriander seeds

1 _____ bunch flat-leaf parsley, about 1 ¾ cups (70 g)

1 cup (240 ml) _____ olive oil

2 tsp (4 g) _____ crushed red pepper

2 _____ garlic cloves

zest _____ of 1 lemon

juice _____ of 2 lemons

to taste _____ salt

2 _____ ciabatta rolls

2 cups (400 g) _ porchetta, warm, thinly sliced and chopped (page 73)

as needed _____ porchetta crackling, roughly chopped (page 73)

to taste _____ dijon mustard

METHOD

To make the salsa verde, toast the fennel and coriander seeds in a dry nonstick skillet over medium heat until fragrant, shaking the pan often, about 2-3 minutes. With a mortar and pestle, grind the fennel seeds and coriander. Add them, along with the parsley, oil, crushed red pepper, garlic, lemon zest and lemon juice, to a blender or food processer and purée until smooth. Taste and season with salt.

Next, toast the buns and then assemble the sandwiches by slicing the rolls lengthwise and topping with porchetta. Add a bit of crackling and a drizzle of salsa verde. Serve with dijon mustard and enjoy immediately.

Note: The salsa verde recipe yields a lot of salsa verde. If you're looking for other uses, it's delicious with pasta or eggs.

SPRING CHICKEN

MAKES: 2

PESTO CHICKEN WITH CELERY, RED PEPPERS & SPRING GREENS

Pesto is super versatile and delicious. It's one of those sauces I'd written off after years of bad store-bought and cheap restaurant versions. After tasting the real thing and then making it fresh at home, I now think it needs to be a staple in everyone's fridge. Stir it into pasta for a quick lunch, or even better, slather it on bread with chicken for a spring-inspired sandwich. I love the herbaceous freshness of pesto with the crunch of vegetables and tender chicken.

INGREDIENTS

2 tbsp (16 g) _____ pine nuts

3 _____ garlic cloves

3 tbsp (45 ml) _____ olive oil

2 tbsp (11.25 g) _____ freshly grated parmesan

1 cup ___ packed basil leaves, roughly chopped

juice _____ of ½ lemon

zest _____ of 1 lemon

to taste _____ salt & freshly ground pepper

2 _____ rolls

1 _____ poached chicken breast
(page 196), thinly sliced

1 _____ celery stalk, sliced on a diagonal

½ _____ red pepper, sliced into strips

1 _____ handful greens of choice

METHOD

Toast the pine nuts in a dry pan over low heat, shaking the pan often until the nuts are golden brown and toasted, about 3-5 minutes. Set aside to cool.

Once the pine nuts are cool, use a mortar and pestle to smash the garlic. Add the pine nuts and continue to grind until everything comes together in a paste. Stir in the oil until well incorporated and then add the cheese and basil. Smash lightly and taste, adding lemon juice, zest and salt and pepper as you see fit.

Toast the buns. Spread 2 tablespoons (30 ml) of pesto on both sides, then layer on the chicken, celery, red pepper and greens. Enjoy immediately.

VIETNAMESE PORK SLIDERS

MAKES: 4

PULLED PORK SANDWICHES WITH PICKLES, PÂTÉ, JALAPEÑOS & CILANTRO

Vietnamese banh mi might possibly be my favorite sandwich of all time. It has cold cuts, pâté, sweet and sour pickled carrots and daikon, fresh cilantro and spicy peppers, all tucked into an ethereally soft yet crispy rice-flour baguette. It all makes for one great sandwich. Sometimes, though, you don't have a Vietnamese deli nearby but you do have a ton of pulled pork, so you go ahead and do what any sane person would do. You make a mash-up of two delicious foods: pulled pork and banh mi.

INGREDIENTS

4	slider buns
2 tbsp	chicken liver pâté (page 195)
2 tbsp (30 ml)	Japanese Kewpie mayo
1 cup (200 g)	pulled pork (page 88), warmed
½ cup (75 g)	quick pickled carrots & daikon (page 64)
8	sprigs cilantro
1	jalapeño, sliced

METHOD

First, toast the slider buns. Then, spread the pâté on the bottom bun and the mayonnaise on the top bun for each sandwich. Top the bottom buns evenly with the pulled pork, carrot and daikon. Add cilantro and jalapeño slices to taste. Add the top bun and serve immediately.

Vietnamese
SLIDERS

PULLED PORK SANDWICHES WITH PÂTE, JALAPEÑOS AND CILANTRO

FRENCH ONION GRILLED CHEESE

MAKES: 2

FRENCH ONION SOUP IN A SANDWICH: CARAMELIZED ONIONS & GRUYÈRE

Grilled cheese is one of the greatest culinary inventions. Crispy, buttery bread sandwiching gooey, melted cheese is one of life's purest pleasures. I started out making grilled cheese sandwiches when I was young with processed cheese between Wonder Bread, but it wasn't long before I was creating all sorts of truly delicious combos. This French onion grilled cheese has sweet, slow-caramelized onions paired with nutty Gruyère. It's a little like eating a French onion soup in sandwich form.

INGREDIENTS

1 tbsp (15 ml)	oil
1	large sweet onion, thinly sliced
2 tbsp (30 g)	butter, room temp
4 slices	bread
1 cup (100 g)	shredded Gruyère
to taste	freshly ground pepper

METHOD

Add the oil and onions to a small saucepan. Stir to coat and cook slowly over medium-low heat, until the onions are caramelized, about 45 to 50 minutes. This is pretty hands-off, but give it a stir every so often.

Butter the bread on one side. Place the bread, buttered side down, on a cutting board and top with ½ of the shredded Gruyère. Top the Gruyère with half of the onions, season with pepper and close the sandwich with another slice of buttered bread, buttered side facing out. Repeat for the second sandwich.

Place the sandwich in a nonstick frying pan over medium heat and grill until golden brown, flipping once, about 4-5 minutes per side. Enjoy immediately.

FRENCH
ONION GRILLED
CHEESE

CHICKEN POT PIE BUN

MAKES: 2

CHICKEN, ONIONS, CARROTS & CELERY IN A CREAMY SAUCE

Fall is the ultimate season for comfort food. Sometimes I'll go out outside just so I can come in from the cold with frozen cheeks and eat something warm and delicious. It's a feeling that can't be beat. This chicken pot pie sandwich is something that I wouldn't mind coming home to after an afternoon of raking leaves. Tender chicken, onions, carrots and celery in a creamy white sauce: it's classic comfort food sandwiched in a warm and crispy bun.

INGREDIENTS

2 tsp (10 ml) _____ oil
¼ cup (40 g) _____ diced onion
¼ cup (40 g) _____ diced carrot
¼ cup (25 g) _____ diced celery
1 tbsp (15 g) _____ butter
1 tbsp (10 g) _____ all-purpose flour
½ cup (120 ml) _____ milk
2 cups (300 g) ____ chopped poached chicken
(page 196)
1 _____ sprig fresh thyme
1 tsp (1.25 g) _____ chopped flat-leaf parsley
to taste _____ salt & freshly ground pepper

2 _____ buns

METHOD

In a medium saucepan, heat the oil over medium heat. Add the onion, carrot and celery and gently cook for 3-5 minutes. Remove vegetables from pan and set aside.

In the same saucepan, melt the butter over medium heat until bubbly. Add the flour and whisk until smooth. Reduce heat to low and cook, stirring occasionally, until it starts to smell nice and toasty, about 2 minutes. Add the milk, stir until smooth and then turn the heat up to medium and cook for 2 minutes until thickened, stirring occasionally. Reduce heat to low and add the vegetables, chicken, fresh thyme and flat-leaf parsley. Taste and season with salt and pepper.

Toast your buns and fill with the chicken filling. Enjoy immediately.

CHICKEN
POT PIE BUN

CHICKEN AND VEGETABLES
IN CREAMY BÉCHAMEL

LAMB
&
PEA
— SANDWICH —

LAMB & PEAS

MAKES: 2-4

BRAISED LAMB WITH MINTY PEAS, CRISPY SHALLOTS & CAPER YOGURT

The best sandwiches are meals in and of themselves. I love taking whole meals and figuring out how to fit them into sandwich form. Anything handheld is definitely better, in my book. A friend once made a lovely Sunday lunch of braised lamb, minted peas and boiled potatoes. It was delicious, but all I could think about was fitting it all into a sandwich so I could take the perfect bite. This is that Sunday lamb all tucked up into a toasty bun.

INGREDIENTS

2 tsp (10 ml) _____ oil

1 lb (450 g) _____ lamb shoulder chop

1 _____ garlic clove, crushed

1 _____ small shallot, chopped

1 _____ carrot, roughly chopped

1 _____ celery stalk, roughly chopped

2 cups (480 ml) _____ beef stock

½ cup (64 g) _____ frozen peas

5 _____ fresh mint leaves, chopped

zest _____ of ¼ lemon

to taste _____ salt & freshly ground pepper

1 tbsp (15 ml) _____ oil

1 _____ shallot, sliced

½ cup (120 ml) _____ yogurt

1 tbsp (12 g) _____ capers

¼ tsp _____ chopped fresh rosemary

to taste _____ salt & freshly ground pepper

2-4 _____ ciabatta rolls

METHOD

In a medium stockpot, heat the oil over medium-high heat. When hot, sear both sides of the lamb until deeply caramelized, about 3 minutes per side. Add the garlic, shallot, carrot, celery and beef stock. Bring to a boil over high heat and then turn down to a bare simmer. Cover and simmer for 1-1 ½ hours or until the lamb is fork tender and falling off the bone.

When the lamb is almost done braising, make the minty pea spread. Bring a small stockpot of water to a boil and add the peas. Cook for 2-3 minutes, drain and mash with a fork. Stir in the mint and lemon zest. Season with salt and pepper to taste.

Heat 1 tablespoon (15 ml) oil in a small frying pan over medium heat. Add the sliced shallots and fry until golden brown and crispy, about 1-2 minutes. Drain on paper towels.

Stir together the yogurt and capers. Set aside.

Remove the lamb from the pot and shred using 2 forks. Add the chopped rosemary, taste and season with salt and pepper. Toast the buns and make the sandwiches. Spread the caper yogurt on the top buns. Divide the lamb equally amongst the bottom buns. Top with minty pea spread and crispy shallots. Place the top bun on and enjoy immediately.

MINI BURGERS

MAKES: 8

SLIDERS WITH SMOKED MOZZARELLA, CARAMELIZED ONIONS & ARUGULA

Basic mini burgers are delicious, but topping them with not-so-basic cheeses, greens and sauces can really give you something to get excited about. This recipe lets you grill up a bunch of mini burgers and then top them with whatever your heart desires. To me, the most important thing is choosing the right buns. Buns are a personal preference, so choose wisely! Don't forget to toast the buns either, as it makes a huge difference in flavor and texture — and if you're feeling extra indulgent, butter them up too.

INGREDIENTS

2 tbsp (30 ml) _____ oil, divided

1 _____ large yellow onion, thinly sliced

1 lb (453 g) _____ ground chuck

as needed _____ salt & freshly ground pepper

8 slices _____ smoked mozzarella

8 _____ slider buns

handful _____ arugula

METHOD

Add 1 tablespoon (15 ml) oil and the onions to a small saucepan. Stir to coat and cook slowly over medium-low heat, until caramelized and cooked, about 45-50 minutes. This is pretty hands-off, but stir every so often.

Divide the meat into 8 equal portions of 2 ounces (56 g) each. Gently shape the beef into patties. Season both sides with salt and pepper.

Heat up the remaining oil in a large heavy skillet or cast-iron pan over high heat until the oil starts to shimmer. Add several patties, being sure not to overcrowd. Cook until deep brown, about 3 minutes and then flip. Add the mozzarella, cover and continue to cook until the burger is cooked through, another 2 minutes.

While the burgers are cooking, toast the buns. Place the burgers on the buns and top with caramelized onions and arugula. Enjoy immediately.

MINI
BURGERS

CURRIED EGG SALAD SANDWICH

CURRIED EGG SALAD

MAKES: 2

A CURRIED TWIST ON CLASSIC EGG SALAD

Egg salad has a rather terrible reputation as 1980s food. I think it's time for an egg salad renaissance though, because egg salad is delicious, especially when done right. I even like my egg salad plain, with just a touch of mayonnaise, salt, pepper and green onions. Add a touch of curry and it's even more irresistible. And, of course, this egg salad tastes best on an equally unfashionable vehicle: soft white bread, ideally toasted on one side only.

INGREDIENTS

2 _____ large eggs, room temp

1 _____ large bowl filled with cold water & ice

½ tsp _____ curry powder

1 tsp (5 ml) _____ dijon mustard

2 tbsp (30 ml) _____ mayonnaise

2 tbsp (10.5 g) _____ sliced green onion

¼ cup (25 g) _____ diced celery

to taste _____ salt & freshly ground pepper

2 slices _____ bread

handful _____ arugula

METHOD

Place the eggs in a small saucepan and cover by at least 1 inch (2.5 cm) of cold water. Bring the water to a boil over high heat. When the water reaches a boil, remove from heat, cover and let sit for 11 minutes. Use a slotted spoon to remove the eggs and immediately plunge them into the ice water bath. Let cool completely. When cool, gently crack and peel the eggs under cold running water.

In a bowl, mix together the curry powder, mustard and mayonnaise. In the same bowl, gently mash the boiled eggs with a fork. Stir in the green onions and celery. Taste and season with salt and pepper. Toast the bread and then spoon curry egg mix on top. Finish with arugula and second slice of toasted bread. Enjoy immediately.

AVOCADO BLT

MAKES: 1

A CLASSIC BLT WITH CREAMY AVOCADO & DJION MUSTARD

A good bacon sandwich is my idea of heaven. Actually, bacon is my idea of heaven, period. Bacon, lettuce and tomatoes are a timeless combination on the level of caprese or carbonara in my book. This sandwich modernizes the timelessness just enough. The creaminess of the avocado, peppery arugula and juicy, sweet tomatoes are all there to accent the rich bacon-ness of bacon. Simply perfect.

INGREDIENTS

2-3 slices	thick-cut bacon
1	mini baguette /roll
to taste	dijon mustard
to taste	mayonnaise
3-4 slices	ripe tomato
½	ripe avocado, sliced
handful	arugula
to taste	salt & freshly ground pepper

METHOD

Lay out bacon slices in a large cold skillet. Turn the heat to medium-low and fry slowly, turning occasionally until the bacon is browned on both sides and most of the fat is rendered out. When brown and crispy, remove from the pan and set on paper towels to absorb excess fat.

Toast the bread and slather one side with mustard and one side with mayonnaise, to taste. Top with the bacon, tomato, avocado and arugula. Season with salt and pepper to taste. Enjoy immediately.

AVOCADO
BACON
LETTUCE
TOMATO

. WARM BEENHAM .

HOT HAM
SPICY MUSTARD
TOASTY BUN

WARM BEENHAM

MAKES: 6

WARM HAM & HOT MUSTARD ON A SOFT BUN

One of my lifelong dreams was to visit the fields of tulips in the Netherlands. I had a vision of me tiptoeing through the endless fields of tulips. Last year I made it to the tulip gardens near Amsterdam, but they don't let you frolic in the massive fields. I was disappointed, but then I saw the food carts selling warm beenhams and my disappointment just melted away. Warm beenhams are basically hot, fried ham and spicy mustard inside the softest white rolls. They totally made up for the lack of dancing.

INGREDIENTS

6 _____ soft white dinner rolls
1 package _____ thinly sliced deli ham
2 tbsp (30 ml) _____ dijon mustard
12 _____ pickle slices

METHOD

Preheat the oven to 300°F (150°C).

Warm the buns in the oven while you are frying the ham.

In a medium frying pan, crisp the ham over medium heat until golden and brown, about 2-3 minutes.

Assemble the sandwich with mustard on both sides of the rolls, then layers of ham and pickle slices. Serve immediately.

HALOUMI CAPRESE

MAKES: 2

FRIED CHEESE WITH RIPE TOMATOES, BASIL & SWEET BALSAMIC

Haloumi is a firm Mediterranean white cheese with a high melting point. It maintains its shape when cooked, which results in crispy golden outsides with meltingly soft insides. It's incredibly delicious and I've been known to fry it up and eat it straight out of the pan. If you have the willpower, after you fry it, put it in these Caprese sandwiches for a delightful twist on an old classic.

INGREDIENTS

¼ **cup (60 ml)** _____ balsamic vinegar

4-6 _____ slices haloumi cheese

2 _____ buns or rolls

as needed _____ olive oil

1 _____ ripe tomato, sliced

6-8 _____ fresh basil leaves, washed & dried

to taste _____ salt & freshly ground pepper

METHOD

In a small saucepan, bring the balsamic vinegar to a boil and then reduce the heat and simmer until it is thick and syrupy, about 2-4 minutes.

Pat the haloumi cheese dry with paper towels. Add to a cold pan, turn the heat up to medium and grill until golden brown, about 3 minutes per side.

Toast your buns or bread and drizzle with the reduced balsamic and some olive oil. Place the grilled haloumi on the bottom slice and top with tomatoes, basil, salt, pepper and bread. Enjoy immediately.

THE

HALOUMI
CAPRESE

SANDWICH

FRIED
Chicken
SLIDERS

FRIED CHICKEN SLIDERS

MAKES: 6

CHICKEN & PICKLES ON A MINI BUN

I'm a big fan of all miniaturized foods, and miniaturized sandwiches in particular, just because they let you trick yourself into eating lots without feeling guilty. Sometimes miniature versions turn out even tastier than the original and these crispy chicken sliders are a perfect example. The tininess of each sandwich means you maximize the crunch of the chicken in every bite.

INGREDIENTS

1 cup	all-purpose flour
2 tsp (6 g)	garlic powder
2 tsp (6 g)	onion powder
½ tsp	paprika
½ tsp	cayenne
½ tsp	salt
½ tsp	freshly ground pepper
1 cup (240 ml)	buttermilk
½ tsp	salt
½ tsp	pepper
2	boneless skinless chicken breasts, cut into six even pieces
as needed	grape seed/rice bran oil
6	slider buns
3 tbsp (45 ml)	mayonnaise
3 tbsp (45 ml)	mustard
12	sliced pickles

METHOD

In a shallow bowl, mix together the flour, garlic powder, onion powder, paprika, cayenne, salt and pepper. In a separate bowl, mix together the buttermilk, salt and pepper. Dip the chicken breast pieces into the flour mix, then buttermilk, then flour again. Rest the coated pieces on a plate while your oil is heating up.

Pour ½ inch (1.3 cm) of oil into a large heavy skillet and heat the oil over medium heat until 350°F (175°C).

Fry the chicken until golden brown and cooked through, about 3-5 minutes per side. Remove from the oil and drain on a rack.

Toast the buns. Spread mustard on the bottom buns and mayonnaise on the top buns. Place one piece of chicken on each bottom bun, then top with pickles and the bun top. Enjoy immediately.

SNACKS

As a kid, I lived for snack time. I think that, back then, part of my love for snacks came from the fact that they meant a little bit of choice when I otherwise couldn't really pick what I ate. The decision between cheese and crackers, celery and carrots, or fruit was wonderfully nerve wracking and could take hours (or so it seemed). Even now, I love snacks because of the choice involved. Snacks give you the chance pick and graze from a huge variety of food. It's definitely worth it, now that I can, to make snacks that are a little more time consuming than just cheese on crackers. Snacks like deep-fried Popcorn Chicken or crispy, crunchy Tuna Yaki Onigiri balls, or creamy, rich Chicken Liver Pâté on toast make the day just that much more special.

POPCORN
×
CHICKEN

SALTY & PEPPERY

POPCORN CHICKEN

SERVES: 3-4

SALTY, PEPPERY DEEP-FRIED CHICKEN BITES

Every culture in the world probably has its own version of fried chicken and I love Taiwan's. Taiwanese night markets are full of street food vendors hawking their wares, and while there are many tempting treats, you'll usually find me in the long line of people patiently waiting for their bag of freshly fried salty, crispy popcorn chicken. I'm never able to stop at just one bag, so to avoid spending long nights in line, I had to learn how to make Taiwanese popcorn chicken at home.

INGREDIENTS

4 _____ boneless skinless chicken thighs

1 tbsp (15 ml) _____ soy sauce

⅛ tsp _____ five spice powder

½ tsp _____ freshly ground black pepper

½ tsp _____ white pepper

1 _____ garlic clove, crushed

1 cup (240 ml) _____ buttermilk

1 cup (120 g) _____ coarse sweet potato starch

1 tsp (2 g) _____ freshly ground black pepper

1 tsp (2 g) _____ white pepper

½ tsp _____ salt

1 tsp (3 g) _____ garlic powder

as needed _____ grape seed/rice bran oil

as needed __ fresh Thai basil leaves, washed & thoroughly dried

½ tsp _____ salt

½ tsp _____ freshly ground black pepper

½ tsp _____ white pepper

⅛ tsp _____ five spice powder

⅛ tsp _____ Sichuan peppercorn powder or crushed red chili flakes

METHOD

Cut the chicken into 1-inch (2.5-cm) pieces. Thoroughly mix the chicken, soy sauce, five spice powder, freshly ground pepper, white pepper, garlic and buttermilk in a large bowl. Marinate for an hour in the fridge.

Mix the sweet potato starch, white and black pepper, salt and garlic powder together in a medium bowl. Take the pieces of chicken, a couple at a time, out of the buttermilk and toss in the coating. Place coated pieces on a baking rack. Rest for 30 minutes.

Preheat the oven to 300°F (150°C). In a deep pot, heat 2 inches (5 cm) oil on medium-high heat until it reaches 350°F (180°C). Set up a wire rack on a large rimmed baking sheet. Fry the chicken in batches until golden brown and crunchy, about 5-6 minutes. When cooked through, drain the chicken on the wire rack. Place the baking sheet in the oven to keep the chicken warm while you continue to fry in batches until all the chicken is cooked.

When all the chicken is cooked, lower the heat so the oil is 300°F (150°C). Add the basil leaves to the oil and fry until bright green, about 30 seconds to 1 minute. Remove and drain on a plate lined with paper towels.

Make the spice mixture by combining the salt, black pepper, white pepper, five spice powder and peppercorns. To serve, top the chicken with the deep-fried basil and a sprinkling of the spice mixture.

HOT
WINGS

SERVES: 2-4

CHICKEN WINGS IN HONEY & SRIRACHA

I knew someone who loved chicken wings so much that he would suffer all sorts of indignities to eat them. As a kid, he was on the chubby side, so in efforts to slim him down, his mom demanded that he run up and down the stairs at least three times per wing before he was allowed to eat. You'd think that this would create some sort of negative association with chicken wings, but no, he still loves wings. I completely understand; wings are universally loved, especially when they're in a sweet and spicy sriracha sauce.

INGREDIENTS

1 tbsp (15 ml) _____ oil

2 tsp (10 ml) _____ sesame oil

¼-½ cup (60-120 ml) _____ sriracha
(adjust according to spice tolerance)

2 tbsp (30 ml) _____ honey

2 tbsp (30 ml) _____ soy sauce

1 tbsp (15 ml) _____ rice vinegar

2 _____ garlic cloves, minced

2 lbs (900 g) _____ chicken wings

as needed _____ oil

METHOD

In a large bowl, mix together the first 7 ingredients. Add the chicken wings and mix well. Marinate in the fridge for 1 hour. Remove the wings from the marinade, reserving the marinade.

If you're cooking indoors, heat a bit of oil in a large nonstick pan over medium to medium-high heat. Add the chicken wings, cover and cook, flipping every so often until cooked through, about 12-15 minutes. Remove the lid, add the remaining marinade and turn the heat up to high to reduce the sauce. Enjoy immediately.

If you're cooking outdoors, when ready to cook, set the grill at medium to medium-high heat. Brush the grill with oil and grill the chicken wings, brushing with the remaining marinade and turning every so often until charred and cooked through, about 14-18 minutes.

Honey Sriracha

HOT
WINGS

Sweet & Spicy

JALAPEÑO POPPERS

MAKES: 12-14

CHICKEN, JALAPEÑOS, CHEDDAR & POTATOES

I like making croquettes whenever I have leftover mashed potatoes. The best thing about leftover mashed potato croquettes is that you can fill them with anything, including other leftovers. These croquettes came about after a roast chicken dinner. There were a bunch of jalapeños in the fridge too, so the leftover potatoes and chicken turned into jalapeño popper croquettes. Creamy and spicy, with a crunchy outer shell, these croquettes may convince you to never settle for regular jalapeño poppers again.

INGREDIENTS

1 cup (210 g) _____ mashed potatoes

1 cup (150 g) _____ shredded poached chicken thighs (page 196)

1-2 _____ jalapeños, minced

¼ cup (21 g) _____ sliced green onions

½ cup (55 g) _____ shredded cheddar

to taste _____ salt & freshly ground pepper

½ cup (70 g) _____ all-purpose flour

1 _____ large egg

1 cup (60 g) _____ panko

as needed _____ grape seed/rice bran oil

METHOD

Thoroughly mix together the mashed potatoes, chicken, jalapeños, green onions and cheddar. Taste and season with salt and pepper.

Shape the potato mixture into small patties. Roll in flour, then egg, then panko.

In a pot with tall sides, heat up 2 inches (5 cm) of oil to 350°F (180°C) over medium heat.

Fry the croquettes in batches until crisp and golden brown, about 4-5 minutes. Place finished poppers on paper towels to drain off excess oil. Enjoy warm.

CRISPY POTATO

JALAPEÑO

POPPERS

CALAMARI & BACON

SERVES: 2-4

CRISPY SQUID & BACON BITES

Madrid is a city for night owls and late night eats, which is perfect for me and Mike. One of our favorite finds was a tiny tapas place that didn't even open its doors until nine at night. By the time we got there at eleven, it was standing room only. We watched as plate after plate of bacon-wrapped calamari served with a squid ink sauce came out of the kitchen. The squid ink captured my attention, but took a backseat to the flavor and texture combination of bacon and calamari. This recipe doesn't have any squid ink and it doesn't need it: the spotlight's on the contrast between the bacon and squid.

INGREDIENTS

1 lb (450 g) _____ calamari strips
1 cup (240 ml) _____ milk
as needed _____ grape seed/rice bran oil
¼ cup (35 g) _____ all-purpose flour
¼ cup (30 g) _____ cornstarch
½ tsp _____ salt
6 _____ slices bacon
to serve _____ lemon wedges

METHOD

Soak the calamari in the milk overnight to soften and tenderize. The next day, remove from the milk and lightly pat dry.

Preheat 2 inches (5 cm) of oil to 350°F (180°C) over medium heat in medium stockpot with tall sides.

In a bowl, mix the flour, cornstarch and salt together. Set aside.

Pat the bacon dry with paper towels and then cut each piece horizontally into 3 long strips. Cut strips in half so you end up with 6 thin strips of bacon per slice.

Tie the bacon strips around several calamari strips. Dip in the flour mixture and deep fry until golden, about 2 minutes. Drain on a wire rack inside a rimmed baking sheet or paper towels and serve immediately with lemon wedges.

TOGETHER

CALAMARI
AND BACON

FOREVER

CHICKEN
LIVER PÂTÉ

CHICKEN LIVER PÂTÉ

MAKES: 2 CUPS

CREAMY, SMOOTH, SAVORY SPREAD

Chicken liver pâté is one of those delicious things that is better left unexplained. Case in point: I once made a batch for a party, where it was quickly devoured. Liver is not universally loved and I was happy people enjoyed it. Imagine my surprise when, later, someone mentioned that he would pass out if he ever ate liver. I didn't say anything but he was the culprit who had eaten the majority of the pâté. Hopefully he's figured out by now that pâté is made from liver and that liver is delicious.

INGREDIENTS

1 lb (450 g)	chicken livers
2	small shallots, minced
2 tbsp (30 g)	butter
⅓ cup (80 ml)	whiskey
¼ cup (60 ml)	heavy cream
½ tsp	salt
⅛ tsp	five spice
¼ tsp	pepper
2	sprigs fresh thyme, leaves only
½ cup (114 g)	butter, melted
to serve	sliced baguette
to serve	crackers
to serve	cornichon
to serve	micro greens
to serve	quince/fig jam

METHOD

Remove any sinew or discolored spots from the livers. Chop into ½-inch (1.3-cm) pieces.

Melt the 2 tablespoons (30 g) of butter in a frying pan over medium-high heat. Add the shallots and liver. Sauté for 2-3 minutes until slightly brown but still rosy inside. Scrape the livers and shallots into a blender or food processor.

Add the whiskey to the pan and boil over high heat until reduced by half. Add the whiskey reduction, cream, salt, five spice, pepper and thyme to the blender. Blend until smooth. Add the melted butter and blend for several seconds. Push the mousse through a fine sieve and pack into jars to chill for 2 hours. Serve with crackers or sliced baguettes, cornichon and fig or quince jam.

CHICKEN SALAD CUPS

SERVES: 2

SHREDDED CHICKEN, FRESH HERBS & CUCUMBERS IN A LETTUCE CUP

I love handheld food in all forms, so I decided to come up with a way to eat salad sans fork. I like to make up a big plate of these and eat them like tacos. The filling of chicken, cilantro, bean sprouts and cucumbers are tossed in a fish sauce vinaigrette that is salty, sweet and addictive. After tasting it, you'll want to toss everything in this vinaigrette. This salad is just as delicious eaten off a plate with a fork, so go ahead and enjoy it either way.

INGREDIENTS

1 _____ clove of garlic

1 _____ Thai chili

5 tbsp (75 g) _____ sugar

1 ¾ cups (420 ml) _____ water

juice _____ ½ lime

¼ cup (60 ml) _____ fish sauce

as needed _____chicken breasts, legs or thighs

as needed _____ salt

juice _____ of 1 lime

zest _____ of 1 lime

4 cups (600 g) ____ shredded poached chicken

½ cup (20 g) _____ cilantro, roughly chopped

½ cup (15 g) _____ packed torn mint leaves

2 _____ green onions, sliced

½ cup (15 g) _____ shiso leaves, torn

½ cup (50 g) _____ bean sprouts

½ cup (50 g) _____ julienned cucumbers

1 head _____ butter lettuce, washed & dried

METHOD

To make the vinaigrette, crush the garlic, chili and sugar together in a mortar and pestle. Add the sugar mixture to the water and stir to dissolve. Add the lime juice, then the fish sauce. Mix thoroughly and refrigerate until needed.

To poach the chicken, place the chicken in a small saucepan and add enough water to cover the chicken by 1 inch (2.5 cm). Add a sprinkle of salt. Bring the water to a full boil over medium-high heat. When the water has come to a rolling boil, turn off the heat and put the lid on. After 15 minutes, remove and slice into a piece of chicken to check for doneness. If pink, return to the pot and cover for 5 more minutes, or until the middle of the chicken is 165°F (74°C). The chicken is cooked when it is uniformly white and opaque with no pink. When cooked, remove the chicken from the pot and cool. Shred or slice as needed.

In a large bowl, mix ¾ cups (165 g) of the prepared fish sauce vinaigrette, lime juice and zest together. Add the shredded chicken, cilantro, mint, green onions, shiso, bean sprouts and cucumbers. Toss until evenly dressed. Taste and season with more fish sauce vinaigrette if needed. Scoop into butter lettuce cups and enjoy immediately.

VIETNAMESE
CHICKEN SALAD
~IN~
LETTUCE CUPS

CURRY CROQUETTES

MAKES: 24 CROQUETTES

DEEP-FRIED POTATO BALLS FILLED WITH MINCED BEEF & PORK CURRY

Japanese korokke is a take on Portuguese croquettes: deep-fried minced meat mixed with mashed potatoes. These korokke have a beef and pork dry curry tucked into the middle. If you're running low on time, you can simply mix the curry into the potatoes before forming the balls and frying.

INGREDIENTS

2 _____ large potatoes, peeled and cubed

2 tsp (10 ml) _____ milk

½ tsp _____ salt

1 tbsp (15 ml) _____ oil

⅛ lb (56 g) _____ ground beef

⅛ lb (56 g) _____ ground pork

½ _____ onion, finely chopped

1 _____ garlic clove, peeled and chopped

1 tbsp (6 g) _____ finely chopped fresh ginger

1 _____ small bell pepper, finely chopped

1 _____ small carrot, finely chopped

1 tbsp (6 g) _____ curry powder

1 tbsp (15 ml) _____ tomato paste

2 tsp (10 ml) _____ Worcestershire sauce

1 tbsp (15 ml) _____ soy sauce

½ tsp _____ freshly ground pepper

1 _____ large egg, lightly beaten

1 cup (60 g) _____ panko

¼ cup (35 g) _____ all-purpose flour

as needed _____ grape seed/rice bran oil

to serve ____ Japanese Kewpie mayo & sriracha

METHOD

Place the potatoes in a pot and cover with cold water. Bring to a boil and simmer until fork tender, 15-20 minutes. Drain, mash with milk and salt and set aside to cool.

In a large skillet, heat oil over medium-high heat. Brown the beef and pork and add the onions, garlic, ginger, peppers and carrots. Stir in the curry powder, tomato paste, Worcestershire sauce, soy sauce and pepper. Taste and adjust if needed. Cool mixture completely.

Once the filling and potatoes are completely cool, make the balls. Scoop 2 tablespoons (40 g) of potato, and flatten. Make a slight indentation in the middle. Scoop in some of the meat filling and fold the potato around the filling while shaping into a ball. Continue to make balls until you run out of potatoes.

Put the beaten egg in a shallow bowl. In another shallow bowl, mix together the panko and flour. Dip the balls into the egg, then the flour and breadcrumb mix. Repeat so that the ball is coated twice, making sure the whole ball is covered in breadcrumbs. Refrigerate the balls for 2 hours minimum.

In a pot with deep sides, heat 3 inches (7.6 cm) of oil to 375°F (190°C) over medium-high heat. Gently lower a few of the balls at a time into the oil and fry until golden brown and crispy, 3-5 minutes, turning occasionally. Drain on paper towels and enjoy warm with Kewpie and sriracha.

Beef
& Pork
CURRY CROQUETTES

PEACH AND BURRATA
WITH
SRIRACHA LIME
DRESSING
PANZANELLA SALAD

SUMMER PANZANELLA

SERVES: 2-4

TOASTED BREAD, RIPE PEACHES & BURRATA IN SRIRACHA LIME DRESSING

The contrasting textures in this salad make it incredibly moreish. The crispy, buttery giant croutons with perfectly soft, ripe peaches and melty, creamy burrata all drizzled with a sweet and sour dressing is fantastic. Cutting into fresh burrata is a joy: the creamy insides ooze out, just asking to be eaten. You can substitute fresh mozzarella, but if you can find burrata, you won't be disappointed.

INGREDIENTS

2 tbsp (30 ml) _____ honey

2 tbsp (30 ml) _____ lime juice

2 tbsp (30 ml) _____ oil

2 tsp (10 ml) _____ sriracha (or to taste)

2 cups (120 g) _____ sourdough bread, cubed in 1-inch (2.5-cm) pieces

1 tbsp (15 ml) _____ oil

2 _____ ripe peaches, sliced

2 (8 oz [227 g]) balls _____ fresh burrata

10-12 _____ fresh mint leaves, torn

to taste _____ salt & freshly ground pepper

METHOD

In a small bowl, whisk the honey, lime juice, oil and sriracha together. Set aside.

Toss the bread in the oil. Heat up a nonstick pan over medium to medium-high heat and toast all sides of the bread cubes until golden brown and crispy.

Cut or tear the burrata into 1-inch (2.5-cm) pieces. In a bowl, toss the bread cubes, peaches, burrata and torn mint leaves in the dressing. Taste and season with salt and pepper. Enjoy immediately.

TUNA YAKI ONIGIRI

MAKES: 4 RICE BALLS

GRILLED SPICY TUNA RICE BALLS

The first time I went to Japan, I was overwhelmed in the best way possible. Jet-lagged, I spent hours in a 7-Eleven, which was nothing like the North American equivalent. It was filled with the ubiquitous, and surprisingly delicious, onigiri, or rice balls. I stood in front of the onigiri display for so long that I was worried I would get kicked out, but the ever-polite Japanese clerk didn't bat an eye. These grilled rice balls are crispy and crunchy, with a spicy tuna surprise in the middle.

INGREDIENTS

1 tsp (5 ml) _____ oil
2 oz (56 g) _____ ahi tuna, cut into ¼-inch (.63-cm) cubes
2 tsp (10 ml) _____ sesame oil
¼ cup (21 g) _____ sliced green onions
2 tsp (10 ml) _____ sriracha
1 tbsp (15 ml) _____ Japanese Kewpie mayo
4 cups (580 g) _____ cooked sushi rice, slightly warm
1 tbsp (15 ml) _____ soy sauce

METHOD

Heat oil in a nonstick pan over medium-high heat. Lightly sear the tuna, about 2-3 minutes. Remove from the heat, let cool and then stir in the sesame oil, green onions, sriracha and Japanese mayonnaise.

Wet your hands and scoop up ½-¾ cups (80-120 g) of rice. Shape rice into a ball and make an indentation in the middle and fill with a spoonful of filling. Cover the filling with a bit more rice and use your hands to compact the rice together, shaping into a triangle.

Or, to shape the rice with a cookie cutter, wet a 2 ½-inch (6-cm) round cookie cutter and place on a cutting board. Scoop ½ cup (80 g) of rice and press down slightly. Add a spoonful of filling and cover with another ½ cup (80 g) of rice. Press down to compact.

Heat a dry nonstick pan over medium heat and grill the rice balls until toasty brown and crisp, about 5-10 minutes per side. Brush with soy sauce and grill again, 1 minute per side. Enjoy warm.

TUNA
YAKI
ONICIRI

CRISPY & CHEWY

OCTOPUS CHIPS

DELICIOUSLY ADDICTIVE

OCTOPUS CHIPS

SERVES: 2-4

LIGHTLY COATED, CRISPY DEEP-FRIED OCTOPUS

I ran into this dish during a late night drinking session at a bar in Vancouver. Octopus can scare some people off, but if you haven't had it before, you should try it. It's similar in texture to calamari, but it's a bit chewier with a slightly different flavor. Octopus covered in a light batter and deep fried is a fun snack when you're looking for something just a bit different.

INGREDIENTS

½ **cup (120 ml)** _____ Japanese Kewpie mayo

2 tsp (10 ml) _____ lemon juice

¼ tsp _____ crushed red pepper

2 tbsp (5 g) _____ chopped cilantro

½ lb (225 g) _____ octopus sashimi, sliced thin

¼ cup (35 g) _____ all-purpose flour

¼ cup (43 g) _____ cornstarch

½ tsp _____ salt

METHOD

Make the lemon chili dip by stirring together the mayonnaise, lemon juice, crushed red pepper and cilantro. Keep in the fridge until ready to use.

In a deep pot, heat 2 inches (5 cm) of oil over medium to medium-high heat until it reaches 370°F (188°C).

Pat the octopus dry with paper towels. In a medium sided bowl, mix together the flour, cornstarch and salt. Add the octopus and stir to coat.

Remove octopus from the flour mixture, shaking off excess.

Add several pieces of coated octopus to the hot oil and deep fry about 30 seconds, until golden and crispy.

Drain on a wire rack or paper towels and serve immediately with lemon chili dip.

Note: You can find sashimi-style octopus at your local Japanese market. Even though it's referred to as "sashimi," the octopus is actually already cooked.

DEEP FRIED

Tofu
FRIES

WITH MISO DRESSING

TOFU
FRIES

SERVES: 2-3

CRUNCHY DEEP-FRIED TOFU WITH MISO TOFU DRESSING

When I was a kid, my mom and I always went grocery shopping at Asian malls. Every week, my mom would choose something different from the food court: Singapore fried rice noodles, creamy congee or barbecue duck and rice. I would always choose deep-fried tofu. Crispy, crunchy, deep-fried tofu was my reward for following my mom around for hours while she searched for the perfect produce. This is my take on deep-fried tofu: French fry-style strips topped with miso-tofu dressing.

INGREDIENTS

3 oz (85 g) _____ soft tofu
2 tbsp (30 ml) _____ shiro miso
2 tbsp (30 ml) _____ rice vinegar
1 tsp (5 ml) _____ sesame oil
½ tsp _____ finely minced ginger

as needed _____ grape seed/rice bran oil
1 block _____ firm tofu

to garnish _____ sliced green onions
to garnish _____ sriracha
to garnish _____ black sesame seeds

METHOD

Preheat the oven to 300°F (150°C).

In a blender or food processor, blend the soft tofu, miso, rice vinegar, sesame oil and ginger until smooth. Set aside while frying the tofu.

Remove the tofu from the package and cut into ¼-inch (.63-cm) strips. Drain the "fries" on paper towels while the oil is heating up.

In a deep pot, heat up 2 inches (5 cm) of oil over medium-high heat until 350°F (180°C). Fry batches of tofu until golden brown and crispy, 7-8 minutes, making sure to stir the fries to prevent them from sticking together. Drain on paper towels and keep warm in oven until all of the tofu is fried.

Top the fries with the miso ginger tofu dressing, green onions, sriracha and black sesame seeds. Enjoy hot.

DESSERT

Dessert really rounds out a meal. It lets you know that you don't need to save any more tummy space, it's time to go all out and indulge. But even though desserts are traditionally an after-meal thing, I actually eat them at all times of the day. No one will judge you if you're up at six in the morning snacking on some bourbon caramel Figs and Cheese cheesecake or if, instead of sitting down to your usual lunch, you decide to have Lemon Meringue S'mores. After all, desserts make the world a happier place — a happier, caramelized banana and ice cream-filled place where you can and should Go Bananas.

CARAMELIZED BANANAS

BANANA ICE CREAM

VANILLA COOKIE CRUNCH

GO
BANANAS

SERVES: 4-6

BANANAS WITH NO-CHURN BANANA ICE CREAM & VANILLA COOKIES

I'm a big fan of desserts that combine hot and cold and this dessert is no exception. I've mentioned before that I'm not a huge fan of single-use kitchen gadgets, but ice cream makers are hard to resist — the idea of making homemade ice cream in any flavor is hugely temping, but the best part of this recipe is that you don't need a bulky ice cream maker. The condensed milk means you don't need to churn your way to homemade smooth, scoopable ice cream.

INGREDIENTS

2 _____ ripe bananas

1 (14 oz [414 ml]) can _____ sweetened
condensed milk

1 tsp (5 ml) _____ vanilla

2 tbsp (30 ml) _____ bourbon

2 cups (480 ml) _____ heavy cream, very cold

½ cup (30 g) ___ vanilla wafer cookies, crushed

2 tbsp (30 g) _____ butter

1 tbsp (15 g) _____ sugar

1 tbsp (4 g) _____ milk powder

2 tbsp (30 ml) _____ honey

1 tbsp (15 ml) _____ water

4 _____ firm bananas,
sliced in half and then lengthwise in thirds

METHOD

Purée bananas in a food processor or blender. Combine the bananas, sweetened condensed milk, vanilla and bourbon in a large bowl.

In a another large bowl, beat the heavy cream with an electric mixer until stiff peaks form. Fold the whipped cream into the banana mixture. Pour into an airtight container and freeze until firm, 6 hours.

While the ice cream is freezing you can make the cookie crunch. Preheat the oven to 250°F (120°C). Toss the cookies, butter, sugar and milk powder together, spread on a lined baking sheet and bake for 20 minutes. Cool and set aside in an airtight container until needed.

When ready to serve your ice cream, make the honey bananas. In a small bowl, whisk the honey and water together. Pour the honey mixture into a large nonstick pan and bring to a boil over medium heat. Arrange the bananas, sliced side down and pan fry until the honey bubbles and caramelizes, 1-2 minutes. Remove from heat. Serve with a scoop of banana ice cream and a sprinkle of vanilla cookie crunch.

VIETNAMESE
COFFEE CAKE
W/CONDENSED MILK FROSTING

COFFEE CAKE

MAKES: 1 (9" [23 CM]) CAKE

VIETNAMESE COFFEE CAKE WITH SWEETENED CONDENSED MILK FROSTING

I've loved coffee ever since my first illicit taste from a forgotten mug left on the countertop. At four years old, I'm pretty sure I was actually in love with the milk and sugar rather than the coffee itself. These days, my favorite way to drink coffee is Vietnamese style: super-dark, intense coffee tempered with sweetened condensed milk. This moist, coffee-filled treat topped with sweetened condensed milk frosting is Vietnamese coffee in a cake.

INGREDIENTS

1 cup (227 g) _____ butter, room temp

1 cup (200 g) _____ sugar

½ cup (110 g) _____ brown sugar

4 _____ large eggs, room temp

2 ¾ cups (385 g) _____all-purpose flour

1 ½ (10 g) tsp _____ baking powder

⅛ tsp _____ salt

¾ cup (180 ml) _____ strong coffee, cooled

¼ cup (60 ml) _____ milk

¾ cups (170 g) _____ butter, room temp

2 cups (320 g) _____ powdered sugar

¼ cup plus 1 tbsp (75 ml) _____ sweetened condensed milk

METHOD

Preheat oven to 350°F (175°C).

First, beat the butter until light and fluffy. Add the sugars and mix until completely incorporated. Add eggs one at a time, beating well after each addition.

In a small bowl, whisk together the flour, baking powder and salt. In a liquid measuring cup, stir together the coffee and milk.

Add a ⅓ of the flour mixture to the butter-sugar mixture and mix until combined. Add ½ of the coffee mixture and mix well. Continue alternating between adding the flour and coffee mixtures, ending with flour.

Pour the batter into a parchment paper-lined 9-inch (23-cm) square pan and bake for 35-40 minutes, or until a toothpick inserted into the center comes out clean.

To make the frosting, beat the butter on medium until light and fluffy. Beat in icing sugar and when smooth, beat in condensed milk until thick and smooth.

Cool cake on a wire rack in the pan completely before icing with the sweetened condensed milk frosting.

MINT
CHOCOLATE CHIP

MAKES: 15 COOKIES

FRESH MINT & DARK CHOCOLATE COOKIES

I have always liked mint and chocolate together. At Christmas time, while everyone was asleep, I used to sneak out to the living room to eat stick after stick of After Eight chocolates until I got sick. These warm chocolate chip cookies with fresh mint are a throwback to one of my favorite childhood treats — without the stomachache. With crisp outsides, a soft and gooey center and a hint of mint, these cookies are best warm.

INGREDIENTS

1 ¾ cups (245 g) _____ all-purpose flour

½ tsp _____ baking soda

¾ tsp _____ baking powder

¼ tsp _____ salt

½ cup plus 2 tbsp (144 g) __ butter, room temp

½ cup plus 1 tbsp (130 g) _____ sugar

½ cup plus 2 tbsp (140 g) _____ brown sugar

1 _____ large egg

1 tsp (5 ml) _____ vanilla extract

¼ cup (7.5 g) fresh mint leaves, finely chopped

1 ½ cups (240 g) _____ dark chocolate chunks

METHOD

Sift the flour, baking soda, baking powder and salt into a bowl and set aside. Cream the butter and sugars until light and fluffy. Add the egg and mix well. Stir in the vanilla extract. Add the dry ingredients and mix until just combined. Stir in the chopped mint and chocolate chunks. Chill in the fridge overnight for best results.

Preheat the oven to 350°F (180°C). Line a baking sheet with parchment paper.

Take 3 tablespoons (45 g) dough at a time and roll into 1 ½-inch (4-cm) balls. Place the balls on the baking sheet at least 2 inches (5 cm) apart. Bake until golden brown but still soft, about 15 minutes. Cool on sheet for 10 minutes then move to rack to cool completely.

CHAI TEA ICE BOX CAKE

MAKES: 1 (9" [23 CM]) CAKE

GRAHAM CRACKERS, CHAI PUDDING & CHOCOLATE WHIPPED CREAM

Ice box cakes are perfect for those days during the summer when it's so hot that you'll do anything to avoid turning on the oven. All you need for this cake is graham crackers, pudding, whipped cream and some fridge time. You can customize this recipe any way you please. If it's too hot to even turn on the stove to cook the pudding, you can always use store-bought. The flavor combinations are endless, but I'm partial to spicy-sweet chai tea with chocolate whipped cream.

INGREDIENTS

⅓ cup (70 g) _____ sugar

2 tbsp (16 g) _____ cornstarch

¼ tsp _____ salt

2 ½ cups (600 ml) _____ whole milk

3 _____ large egg yolks

2 tbsp (30 g) _____ butter, cut into small pieces

1 tsp (5 ml) _____ vanilla

2 _____ chai tea bags

2 tsp (10 g) _____ sugar

¼ cup (25 g) _____ unsweetened cocoa powder

2 cups (480 ml) _ cold whipping cream, divided

32 _____ graham crackers

METHOD

Set a fine mesh strainer over a bowl. In a cold saucepan, whisk together the sugar, cornstarch and salt. Slowly drizzle in the milk while whisking, making sure you dissolve the cornstarch. Whisk in the egg yolks. Cook over medium heat while whisking until the pudding starts to thicken and bubble, 5-6 minutes. Reduce to medium-low and stir, using a rubber spatula to scrape the bottom and sides. When pudding is thick and falls back into visible ribbons when drizzled, it's done, about 3-5 minutes. Remove from the heat and stir in the butter and vanilla. When the butter is completely incorporated, pour pudding through the mesh strainer. Press a piece of saran wrap directly onto the pudding and chill for 2 hours.

Brew 1 bag of chai tea in 3 tablespoons (45 ml) of hot water. When cool, squeeze out tea bag and discard. Cut open remaining tea bag and pulse in a food processor until fine. When the pudding is cool, stir in the prepared tea and tea leaves.

Make the chocolate whipped cream: sift the sugar and cocoa. Mix with ¼ cup (60 ml) of cream until incorporated. Stir in remaing cream. Chill for 1 hour. Whip until medium-soft peaks form.

In the bottom of a 9-inch (23-cm) square pan, spread a thin layer of pudding. Lay down crackers and evenly spread a layer of pudding on top. Place another layer of graham crackers and top with chocolate whipped cream. Repeat until you have 5 layers of crackers. Cover and set in the fridge overnight before serving.

CHAI TEA

ICE BOX

CAKE

DOUBLE ALMOND COOKIES

MAKES: 18 COOKIES

CRISP AND CHEWY ALMOND COOKIES

Twice-baked almond croissants are so popular at my local bakery that you have to preorder them first thing in the morning or be disappointed when you drop by and find them croissant-less. Not one to plan ahead, I had this happen to me one too many times so I decided to take matters into my own hands. Unfortunately, waiting for croissant dough to proof is by no means fast, so I came up with a soft and chewy double almond cookie alternative to give me a quick dose of that almond texture and taste I love.

INGREDIENTS

1 cup (140 g) _____ all-purpose flour

½ tsp _____ baking soda

¾ tsp _____ baking powder

½ tsp _____ salt

½ cup (114 g) _____ butter, room temp

½ cup (100 g) _____ sugar

½ cup (110 g) _____ brown sugar

¾ cup (115 g) _____ almond flour

1 _____ large egg

1 tsp (5 ml) _____ almond extract

1 cup (100 g) _____ almonds, roughly chopped

½ cup (50 g) _____ sliced almonds

as needed _____ powdered sugar

METHOD

Preheat the oven to 350°F (180°C). Line a baking sheet with parchment paper.

Sift the all-purpose flour, baking soda, baking powder and salt into a bowl and set aside. Cream the butter, sugars and almond flour until light and fluffy. Add the egg and mix well. Stir in the almond extract. Add the dry ingredients and mix until just combined. Stir in the chopped almonds.

Take 2 tablespoons (30 g) dough at a time and roll into a ball. Flatten slightly and sprinkle with sliced almonds. Refrigerate for 1 hour to prevent cookies from spreading too much during baking.

Bake until golden brown but still soft, about 12 minutes. Cool on sheet for 10 minutes, then move to rack to cool. Dust with powdered sugar and enjoy.

FRESH FROM THE OVEN

DOUBLE
ALMOND
COOKIES

ALMOND FLOUR & PIECES

RASPBERRY
PISTACHIO
PAVLOVA

RASPBERRY PISTACHIO PAVLOVA

MAKES: 14 MINI PAVLOVAS

PISTACHIO MERINGUE, RASPBERRIES & WHIPPED CREAM

One September, I had the pleasure of celebrating my birthday in Paris. My birthday treat of choice was a raspberry pistachio pastry from acclaimed pastry chef Pierre Hermé. This is a super simplified version of my birthday tart: pistachio meringue, ripe raspberries and softly whipped cream.

INGREDIENTS

2	large egg whites
⅛ tsp	salt
½ cup (100 g)	sugar
1 tsp (4 g)	cornstarch
¼ tsp	vanilla
½ tsp	white wine vinegar
¼ cup (30 g)	pistachios, roughly chopped
½ cup (120 ml)	whipping cream, whipped into soft peaks
1 cup (125 g)	raspberries
to serve	chopped pistachios

METHOD

Preheat the oven to 350°F (180°C).

With an electric mixer, whip the egg whites with the salt until peaks start to form. Add the sugar in a slow stream. Continue to whip until the eggs are shiny and stiff. Sprinkle in the cornstarch, vanilla, vinegar and pistachios. Gently fold to combine.

Scoop the meringue into equal mounds on a parchment-lined baking sheet. Place in the oven and immediately turn down to 300°F (150°C) and bake for 25 minutes. Turn the oven off and leave in for another 25 minutes and then remove from the oven. Cool completely.

To serve, top with softly whipped cream, raspberries and an extra sprinkle of chopped pistachios.

Note: If you want super-green pistachios, blanch them in boiling water for 10-15 seconds. Strain, then rub with a clean tea towel to remove their skins. If the skins are still clinging, keep the pistachios in cold water as you rub.

LONDON FOG TEA CAKE

MAKES: 1 (9-INCH [23-CM]) CAKE

EARL GREY & VANILLA SPONGE CAKE

I love tea and usually take it black (opposite of how I drink coffee), but one day a good friend introduced me to the deliciousness of London Fogs. London Fogs are made with Earl Grey tea, steamed milk and vanilla syrup. I was immediately obsessed with the creamy flavor combination and came up with this cake not long after my first taste. This cake is light, fluffy and, if you have it alongside a London Fog, it pleasantly intensifies the experience.

INGREDIENTS

3 _____ Earl Grey tea bags

¾ cup (180 ml) _____ hot water

5 _____ large egg yolks

2 tbsp (30 g) _____ sugar

⅓ cup (80 ml) _____ oil

1 tsp (5 ml) _____ vanilla

¼ tsp _____ salt

1 ⅓ cup (130 g) _____ cake flour

¾ tsp _____ baking powder

5 _____ large egg whites

¼ cup plus 2 tbsp (80 g) _____ sugar

2 cups (480 ml) _____ whipping cream

2 tbsp (30 g) _____ sugar

1 tsp (5 ml) _____ vanilla

METHOD

Preheat the oven to 325°F (170°C). Line the bottom of a 9-inch (23-cm) square pan with parchment paper. Steep 2 of the tea bags in the hot water for 10 minutes. Remove the bags, squeezing out as much liquid as possible. Cool the tea completely.

In a large bowl, beat the egg yolks and 2 tablespoons (30 g) sugar until thick and pale. Slowly drizzle in the oil and continue to beat until completely incorporated. Pour in the cooled tea, the tea leaves from 1 bag of tea, vanilla and salt. Gently mix in the cake flour and baking powder.

In another large bowl, beat the egg whites until foamy. Gradually pour in ¼ cup plus 2 tablespoons (80 g) sugar while beating until stiff peaks form. Gently fold the egg whites into the flour mixture in thirds. Pour the batter into the pan and lightly tap it on the counter top to remove air bubbles.

Bake for 30 minutes or until a toothpick comes out clean. Keep the cake in the pan and invert on a wire rack to cool for 1 hour before flipping back to cool completely right side up.

Make the vanilla whipped cream: whisk the cream on medium-high until it starts to thicken. Reduce to medium and pour the sugar in slowly. Whisk until soft peaks form, then add the vanilla and whisk until stiff peaks form.

To serve, slice the cake and serve with a dollop of vanilla whipped cream on the side.

VANILLA
EARL GREY
TEA CAKE

LEMON
MERINGUE
S'MORES

LEMON MERINGUE S'MORES

MAKES: UP TO 16 S'MORES

TOASTED MARSHMALLOWS, LEMON CURD & GRAHAM CRACKERS

I love lemons and can eat lemon curd by the spoonful. I often have a jar just sitting in the fridge, waiting for a moment of weakness. One day I had a fresh batch of marshmallows begging to be made into s'mores, but I couldn't find any chocolate. I looked in my fridge for inspiration, saw the lemon curd and went for it. These s'mores remind me of lemon meringue pie: the toasty golden brown of the marshmallows go wonderfully with the tartness of the lemon curd and the crunch of graham crackers.

INGREDIENTS

2 tbsp (14 g or 2 envelopes)	gelatin
1 cup (240 ml)	cold water, divided
2 cups (400 g)	sugar
¼ tsp	salt
2 tsp (10 ml)	vanilla extract
as needed	powdered sugar
¼ cup (57 g)	butter, room temp
4	large egg yolks
½ cup (100 g)	sugar
¼ tsp	salt
⅓ cup (80 ml)	lemon juice, about 2 large lemons
zest	of 1 lemon
32	graham crackers

METHOD

To make the marshmallows, spray a 9-inch (23-cm) square pan with non-stick spray and lightly dust with powdered sugar. In a small bowl, soak the gelatin in ½ cup (120 ml) cold water. Set aside. Put ½ cup (120 ml) water and sugar in a pot and stir to dissolve over medium heat. Add the gelatin water and bring to a boil. Remove from the heat and pour into the bowl of an electric mixer. Let stand for 5 minutes. Stir in the salt and vanilla.

Beat with an electric mixer on low for 2 minutes, then increase to high, continuing to whip until soft and doubled in volume, about 10-15 minutes. Pour into the prepared pan and smooth with an spatula. Cool uncovered in the pan, 3 hours. Cut into squares and dust with powdered sugar.

To make the lemon curd, in a heavy-bottomed saucepan, cream the butter, egg yolks and sugar together. Add the salt, lemon juice and zest and mix well. Place the saucepan over low heat and stir frequently with a heatproof spatula. Cook until curd starts to thicken, 12-15 minutes. It's done when you coat the back of your spatula, run your finger through it, and it leaves a clear path. Pour the curd through a fine mesh strainer and refrigerate until needed.

To make the s'mores, preheat the oven to 400°F (205°C). Lay down 16 graham crackers, or as many as desired. Top with lemon curd and marshmallows. Bake until the marshmallows are puffy and golden, about 3-5 minutes. Remove from the oven and top with more curd and graham crackers. Enjoy immediately.

FIGS & CHEESE CHEESECAKE

MAKES: 1 (9-INCH [23-CM]) CAKE

CHEESECAKE WITH A DRIED FIG GRAHAM CRUST & BOURBON CARAMEL

Cheesecakes are straight up dangerous. You'll find yourself in bed at three o'clock in the morning, thinking about how there are three more slices in the fridge, just begging you to eat them. In this cheesecake, the figs give the graham crust a sweetness and slight crunch. You might be tempted to skip making the bourbon caramel sauce, but don't, the caramel adds a depth and dimension that contrasts perfectly with the creaminess of the cheesecake.

INGREDIENTS

1 ½ cups (135 g) _____ graham cracker crumbs

¼ cup (70 g) _____ finely chopped dried Black Mission figs

6 tbsp (90 g) _____ melted butter

2 (8 oz [225 g]) packages _____ cream cheese, room temp

1 cup (200 g) _____ sugar

3 _____ large eggs

2 tsp (10 ml) _____ vanilla extract

1 cup (200 g) _____ sugar

¼ cup (60 ml) _____ water

½ cup (120 ml) _____ heavy cream

2 tbsp (30 ml) _____ bourbon

to taste _____ flaky sea salt

METHOD

Preheat the oven to 350°F (180°C). Line a 9-inch (23-cm) square pan with parchment paper.

Stir together the graham cracker crumbs, figs and butter. Press into the bottom of the pan. Bake for 8-10 minutes. Remove and let cool completely. Turn the oven down to 300°F (150°C).

Blend cream cheese and sugar in a food processor or stand mixer until smooth and creamy. Add eggs 1 at a time, continuing to blend until well incorporated. Spread batter evenly over the cooled crust. Bake until set but still jiggly in the center, 45 minutes. Place on a cooling rack and cool completely in pan and then chill in the fridge until firm, 2 hours.

While the cheesecake is chilling in the fridge, make the bourbon caramel sauce. In a small saucepan, without stirring, simmer the sugar and water over medium heat until a deep amber color.

Remove from the heat and slowly add the heavy cream while stirring. Add the bourbon and place back on low heat while stirring for 1 minute. If not using immediately, transfer to a heatproof dish and store in the fridge. Warm over low heat before using.

When ready to serve, slice cheesecake into squares, top with bourbon sauce and sprinkle of sea salt.

GRAHAM FIG CRUST

FIGS & CHEESE

BOURBON CARAMEL SAUCE

ABOUT STEPHANIE LE

Stephanie used to be a very picky eater until she became someone
who ate everything. She has a soft spot for things that go moo,
noodles, potatoes, travel and the home life.

She cooked through the entirety of the Momofuku cookbook
and now blogs at iamafoodblog.com where she cooks and
photographs random foods that tickle her fancy.

ACKNOWLEDGMENTS

This book wouldn't have been possible without the following:

To Page Street Publishing Co., especially Will, Meg B. and Marissa. Thank you for making one of my wildest dreams come true and for having faith in my writing, photography and design skills. I couldn't ask for a better publishing house.

To my parents, for showing me what good food was even when I didn't want to eat it. Dad, you showed me what it means to be fearless in the kitchen – even though you still don't know how to make steamed sponge cake, you claim you do, and both your fearlessness to fail and ability to learn from it are lessons well learned. Mom, thank you for making me peel all those shallots when I was young. I hardly ever cry when peeling onions now, and I think it's because my eyes were trained at an early age. Thank you for letting me watch while you cook—you're the reason I'm not scared of deep frying.

Kevin, thank you for being the quintessential big brother and always sharing the last bite, even when you want it for yourself. Kim, you introduced me to Ataulfo mangos, the joy of Starbucks and so many delicious Vietnamese delicacies. Thank you for becoming such an integral part of our family. Isaac, your favorite food happens to be mine as well— we are noodle folk together! And to the little bean who hasn't been born yet—you are already well loved and soon you will be well fed.

To Sophie, Amy, Nora and Judy: thanks for your support in all that I do. To Bruce and Betty: thank you just for being you. I couldn't wish for better friends. Minna, thank you for all your advice over the years, but please, when are you going to share your mom's famous vegetarian pho recipe?

To the readers of I Am a Food Blog, thank you from the bottom of my heart. I write posts thinking that no one ever reads them, but you keep coming back for more. I can't thank you enough!

And, of course, the most sincere thanks to Mike. In so many ways, this wouldn't have been possible without you. Thank you for your patience and unwavering faith; for letting me dream and showing me that dreams can become reality; and for having conversations with me at four in the morning about the merits of browning meat before braising, or whether or not sriracha really goes with eggs. Essentially, thank you for being you.

INDEX